THE TRUTH WITHIN THE LIE

THE TRUTH WITHIN THE LIE

How to Align with Universal Principles to Create the Life You Deserve

Dana Grant

©2025 All Rights Reserved. No portion of this book may be reproduced, stored in a retrieval system, or transmitted in any form or by any means—electronic, mechanical, photocopy, recording, scanning, or other—except for brief quotations in critical reviews or articles without the prior permission of the author.

Published by Game Changer Publishing

Paperback ISBN: 978-1-967424-66-5

Hardcover ISBN: 978-1-967424-67-2

Digital ISBN: 978-1-967424-68-9

www.GameChangerPublishing.com

READ THIS FIRST

Just to say thanks for buying and reading my book,
I would like to connect with you!

Scan the QR Code Here:

*For Danielle, Jessica, and Claire.
My beloved daughters,*

*This is for you—the ones who stood by me when I was still finding my way.
The ones who endured the chaos, the confusion, and the pain. You didn't get
the healed version of me, but you loved me through
the unhealed parts anyway.*

*Thank you for your strength, your grace, and for teaching me
what unconditional love truly means.*

This book is a piece of that healing and it's yours.

*With all my love,
– Mom*

ADVANCE PRAISE

"In *The Truth Within the Lie*, Dana Grant shares hard-won wisdom from her personal healing journey. Her compassionate storytelling and intuitive reflections offer readers a supportive space to examine their own emotional patterns, reconnect with inner truth, and reclaim their inherent worth."

~ Terri Cole, Psychotherapist, Bestselling Author,
Host of *The Terri Cole Show*

"Dana Grant is the real deal—and this book? It's like sitting down with your wisest, most grounded friend who also isn't afraid to call you on your crap. *The Truth Within The Lie* will shake up everything you thought you knew about your limits, your worth, and your potential. If you're ready to stop outsourcing your power and start living in full alignment with truth, this is your permission slip."

~ Andrea Owen, author of *How to Stop Feeling Like Sh*t*

"What if the stories you've been told about your worth—your potential, your safety, your success—were all lies? And what if the truth has been inside you all along, waiting to be remembered? In The Truth Within the Lie, transformational coach Dana Grant takes you on an unflinching, empowering journey through her own trauma and triumph, revealing how the 14 Universal Laws can help you realign your energy, reclaim your power, and rewrite the story of your life. Raw, relatable, and radically honest, this is a book for anyone ready to stop surviving and start consciously creating the life they actually deserve."

~ Laura Gassner Otting, Wall Street Journal Bestselling Author of *Wonderhell*

"Dana Grant has cracked the code on transformational living. In *The Truth Within The Lie*, she bridges ancient universal wisdom with real-life application in a way that's both soul-stirring and results-driven. This isn't just a book—it's a roadmap to alignment, purpose, and unstoppable success. If you're ready to rise, this is your launchpad."

~ Dr. Greg S. Reid, Award-Winning Author, Speaker, Filmmaker

"Dana's book is the friend you want by your side to help you on this journey in shifting from old patterns to new patterns! From stuck to unstuck from limiting beliefs to true abundance."

~ Darleen Santore, "Coach Dar"

"*The Truth Within the Lie* is a powerful testament to the healing that becomes possible when we face our stories head-on. With unflinching honesty, deep insight, and fierce compassion, Dana Grant shows us how to turn pain into purpose, reclaim our truth, and realign with our worth. This book is both a mirror and a roadmap—a soul-stirring guide for coming home to yourself."

~ Nancy Levin, author of *The Art of Change*

"This book is soul medicine. Dana Grant lays it all out—grief, trauma, healing, truth—and guides you through the universal laws with raw honesty and radiant power. *The Truth Within the Lie* is a must-read for every woman who's ready to reclaim her energy, rewrite her story, and remember that she is the damn miracle. Dana, thank you for this masterpiece. I'll be recommending it far and wide."

~ Susan Hyatt, Master Certified Life Coach
and Bestselling Author of *BARE*

"This book is a masterpiece and a breathtaking testament to the resilience of the human spirit and the power of self-discovery. With fearless honesty, Dana unpacks the echoes of early trauma and the ways we search for safety in a chaotic world. She reveals that true healing isn't about erasing the past—it's about honoring every version of ourselves with unwavering compassion and grace. This book is a powerful invitation to turn pain into purpose and reclaim the deepest truths that live within us all."

~ Amberly Lago, USA Today Bestselling Author,
TEDx Speaker, Coach, and Podcast Host

THE TRUTH WITHIN THE LIE

HOW TO **ALIGN** WITH **UNIVERSAL PRINCIPLES** TO CREATE **THE LIFE YOU DESERVE**

DANA GRANT

FOREWORD

by Dr. Yasmine Saad, Ph.D
Top 3 NYC Psychologist | Creator of the Inner Message Approach® | TEDx Editor's Pick Speaker

There are books that teach. There are books that inspire. And then there are books that wake you up. Not with noise or urgency—but with clarity. With truth. With presence.

Dana Grant's *The Truth Within the Lie* is that kind of book.

From the very first page, Dana invites us into the heart of her story—not to dwell in the past, but to use it as a gateway for transformation. She writes with disarming honesty, vulnerability, and insight that can only come from someone who has walked through fire and emerged not bitter, but beautifully awake.

As a psychologist and the creator of the Inner Message Approach®, I have spent my career helping people decode the stories they tell themselves—especially the painful ones they inherited, absorbed, or created in order to survive. The negative thoughts that loop in our minds often carry a misunderstood purpose. They are not here to sabotage us—they're here to wake us. To point us toward unmet needs, buried truths, and unclaimed parts of ourselves. Dana's book is a living embodiment of that philosophy. She doesn't just speak about healing—she shows us, with raw elegance, how it unfolds.

In this book, Dana takes us law by law—through the foundational principles that govern both our emotional and energetic lives. From the Law of Vibration to the Law of Forgiveness, each chapter offers more than insight—it offers integration. Through stories of trauma, success, shame, love, and awakening, she walks us through the energetic imprints we carry, often unknowingly, and gives us the tools to transmute them into power. Not performative power—but soul-aligned presence.

What's especially remarkable is Dana's ability to make the mystical feel accessible and the emotional feel actionable. She bridges what we know psychologically—that we recreate what feels familiar, even when it hurts—with what we sense spiritually: that there is something greater moving through us, calling us back to who we truly are.

This book will meet you where you are. If you are in a moment of unraveling, it will feel like a hand on your back. If you are in a chapter of rebuilding, it will remind you that strength does not come from pushing harder, but from listening more deeply. If you are thriving and seeking meaning, it will deepen your connection to your truth, your energy, and your inner compass.

Dana reminds us that the lies we carry—"I'm not enough," "I don't deserve love," "I'll never be safe"—are not flaws in our psyche, but portals. Each one contains the seed of its own healing. When we stop fighting our emotions and begin decoding them, we access the intelligence beneath the pain. That's when everything changes—not from the outside in, but from the inside out.

This is more than a self-help book. This is a soulful journey back to the truest, most empowered version of you.

Dana's story is her own—but the resonance is universal. In sharing it, she gives every reader permission to embrace theirs, no matter how imperfect or painful it may be. That is the power of this work: it liberates us from shame, reconnects us to worth, and gently reminds us that we were never broken—only buried under beliefs that were never ours to begin with.

So, take a breath. Open these pages. And prepare not just to learn—but to remember. To remember the truth that lives beneath every lie you've ever believed. You are worthy. You are powerful. You are whole. And this book will help you live like it.

With deep respect and resonance,

~ Dr. Yasmine Saad

CONTENTS

Introduction	xxi
I Have Been A Thousand Different Women	xxiii
1. The Candy Connection *The Law of Perpetual Transmutation of Energy*	1
2. You're Not Enough (You Never Will Be) *The Law of Vibration*	17
3. Everything Is Connected *The Law of Abundance*	35
4. The Brutal Balancer *Universal Law of Polarity*	51
5. We Don't Always Get What We Want, But We Get What We Need *The Law of Attraction*	65
6. Universal Law of Alignment *The Awakening*	77
7. Law of Cause and Effect *The Headaches, the Medication, the Legs*	91
8. Do You Believe You're Worth It? *The Law of Compensation*	101
9. Are You Ready to Let Go? *The Law of Sacrifice*	115
10. Can I Be Connected to Both? *Law of Relativity*	137
11. Body Balance *Universal Law of Masculine and Feminine*	151
12. Are You Ready? *The Law of Success*	165
13. It Starts and Stops Here *The Law of Forgiveness*	187
14. The Redwood Effect *The Law of Divine Oneness*	203
Conclusion	223
Thank You For Reading My Book!	225

INTRODUCTION

Writing this book has taken me a lifetime of pain, grief, joy, and experiences that I couldn't have anticipated. My desire to share pieces of my life and what helped me evolve is my passion and evolution, and perhaps, my reason for being here is to pay it forward.

I've incorporated many modalities and tools, as no one path brought me here. I certainly know that healing is not linear. Hopefully, you'll be able to embrace this process, taking what you need and leaving the rest behind.

I want to express my deep gratitude to everyone who walked this path with me, especially through the deep grief and betrayals. If not for those experiences, I wouldn't be paying this forward now.

This evolution is full circle. I hope that you are able to see yourself in my story, take what you need, and pay it forward.

I HAVE BEEN A THOUSAND DIFFERENT WOMEN

BY EMORY HALL

*make peace
with all the women
you once were.*

*lay flowers
at their feet.*

*offer them incense
and honey
and forgiveness.*

*honor them
and give them
your silence.*

listen.

*bless them
and let them be.*

*for they are the bones
of the temple
you sit in now.*

*for they are
the rivers
of wisdom
leading toward
the sea.*

CHAPTER 1
THE CANDY CONNECTION
THE LAW OF PERPETUAL TRANSMUTATION OF ENERGY

"Just as a caterpillar transforms into a butterfly, we can transmute our negative experiences into positive growth."
~ Dana Grant

When we are born, we come into the world with two fundamental fears: the fear of loud noises and the fear of falling. As a five-year-old with an alcoholic father and a mother who was deeply in survival mode, there was not a lot of nurture and understanding for me.

I recognize now that my dad suffered from his alcoholism and paid it forward to me—because of his suffering, I have never touched alcohol. That deep gratitude is how I shift into a high vibrational energy today.

However, at the time, the only thing that five-year-old me was aware of was that I was looking for safety. Before my parents divorced, we lived in an upper-middle-class neighborhood in Pleasanton, California. I remember wandering around a lot by myself. I think back in the '70s there was a lot of freedom to do that as a child, not like today. I remember having to be home for dinner time.

In the birth order, I was number four and there were five children within seven years. My younger brother and I were "Irish Twins," which means we were the same age for six weeks out of the year. Perhaps you can imagine the amount of chaos happening at the same time. I found my escapism early on from the wonderment of Barbie and her Barbie van. My earliest memories are of my father driving a delivery truck that was filled with cigarettes and candy, routinely bringing me a cinnamon lollipop as I played with the Barbies under the green plum tree in the backyard in my little white blouses and plaid skirts. I remember this viscerally. In fact, in writing this book, I found a candy store that sold them and kept them on my desk throughout this process.

Why do I share all the little details of my father being the "Candyman" and the plum tree in the backyard? Because everything is connected. My love for cooking and canning plum jelly, to this day, is a huge part of my life. I was addicted to sugar for years. In high school, when I played the violin, I would fill my violin case with fruity candies, especially cinnamon and green apple Jolly Ranchers. Even now, when I'm stressed, I will buy them.

I remember the neighborhood boy asked to see my underwear, and in exchange, he would show me his. I lifted my little cotton dress, and he showed me his. When I told my mom about it at dinner that night, I was spanked and sent to bed without dinner. That was my first interaction with shame, and it stayed with me for the rest of my life.

My mom called me a prude, as I was very protective of my body in my teenage years and, to be honest, very frightened. I might have been the last virgin to graduate in 1982! Looking back on it now, I can see the story I created and where it started. Can something as simple as a spanking and shaming me for showing my little flower underpants at age five do this? Absofuckinglutely.

My parents divorced in '71 and remarried quickly. I had a very unkind stepfather. My mom would say he was super intelligent and didn't have time to be emotionally connected. He lacked empathy and kindness, and he would mock me and say that I would never become anything in the world. My mom claims that she told me I could do anything, and my dad used to call me "Miss America." So, which was true? The pendulum swung back and forth for years.

Believe it or not, our subconscious is responsible for 95% of how we show up in the world, and 85% of what we remember is negative. At the time, I didn't have the tools or practices to handle this in a healthy way, but I did learn how to survive. I created stories that protected me, and I found ways to avoid uncomfortable situations.

I lived in a world of chaos and gaslighting, and I learned to second-guess my experiences. This could be as simple as me telling my mother the truth about the experience I had with my stepfather and her replying, "You know that's not true," painting the picture that I was a pathological liar. I was sold out emotionally on a consistent basis. She never honored how I felt, and there was no space held for my truth.

I also learned to fight, and I dug my feet in so I could be heard. The fact is that I was never heard and honored. That set up my reality for the next 40 years.

It wasn't until I was in my late 40s and my life epically fell apart—and we'll get to that later—that I began my healing journey and decided to make some radical changes. I would've died if I had continued on the same path.

Did I wear rose-colored glasses to survive? Absolutely. Did I live in my own world? Absolutely. Did I need to be safe? Absolutely, and that required me to have a belief system that my inner five-year-old child was running the show even into my 40s without any knowledge from me.

So, what does all this have to do with the law of perpetual energy? Every experience we've ever had, we are exchanging with another. And every experience I had, I was exchanging with the five-year-old who was traumatized.

Trauma can show up in lots of different ways. I learned how to be extraordinarily protective, but I also sought external approval. I was a people-pleaser, and I did not know how to hold safety in my body. I looked outside of myself to find safety and, believe it or not, I was 50 years old before I understood that home and safety lived within me.

I had a huge awakening eight years ago when I realized that every time I drove to my mom's ranch, I would pull into the dollar store. You know the ones—where you can buy a big package of candy for a dollar. I would spend $35 on candy, like Boston Baked Beans, fruity candies, and even chocolate, which is not really my vibe, but I would grab it all. When I checked out, they would always say, "Are you having a party?" and I would lie and say, "Yes." That was my safety. I would buy that and put it in the backseat of my car and never, ever eat it.

I no longer do that, but the realization that I did it because I did not feel safe when I went without it rocked my world. I remember pulling over to the side of the road and sobbing for the grown woman who never understood what that box of candy meant. Did that cinnamon lollipop represent safety from my mom's rage? From her yelling? From her anger? From my father's alcoholism? My five-year-old self thought so.

I will still go to the airport and buy some fruit candies on my way to a speaking engagement. Just in case, right? I usually never touch it, and I'm very aware of why I'm doing it. The truth is that comfort habits die hard. We're not looking for perfection. It's not even obtainable, but I celebrate where I am and who I am, and I love every version of me, especially the one that filled her violin case up with Sweet Tarts.

And if you are asking, yes, I was first chair violin—and first chair clarinet, too. I spent hours practicing in my room. I got to eat my candy, and it was safe.

THE TRUTH WITHIN THE LIE

THE LIE: *I need emotional regulation, and I wasn't able to trust the people or experiences around me.*

THE TRUTH: *I wasn't taught to trust relationships or myself.*

The result of believing the lie was years of using sugar to manage my emotions.

You are born worthy. It is your birthright. The heart doesn't ask questions of worthiness. It just is, and it expands.

I came into this world, and I understood that I needed to survive. I didn't connect with my worthiness, even though I should have known I was worthy. Energetically, we only go as high as our worthiness and how we feel.

What you transmute in energy, you will get back, and I say this knowing that I attracted a lot of betrayal and lack of safety. Now, I was a safe person, and I didn't betray anyone, but guess what? This is where the perpetual cycle is in the law of energy.

I betrayed myself. I didn't feel safe with myself. This is your relationship with you that expands out.

Our energy goes 15 feet out in all directions when we walk into a room. Sometimes, we say, "I don't know what it is about that person. It's an energy thing."

Well, guess what? It is an energy thing. Everything is energy. What we transmute out, we get back in.

So, even though I didn't betray people, I called that in because I betrayed myself. I didn't find the safety within, so I constantly abandoned myself. That feeling was at the core of my experience, but when I was able to shift, everything shifted with me.

You can change your energy by what you put out, but your relationship with you has to change first.

Energy is always moving. It's never stagnant. It's never stuck. Instead, it moves, ebbs, and flows with everything in your life. If you don't understand that energy is in a state of perpetual transformation, you can't fully surrender and access its power.

Now, let me explain a little bit more about that. Earlier, I said that being born worthy is your birthright. Everything about you being brought into the world is perfect. Everything after that, however, you adapt, you take on.

Think of it this way: when you get hurt or something doesn't go right, you become reactive and protect yourself by putting on pieces of armor. The world is giving you a story that you are now reacting to. Energy is how you show up. So, if we believe life is fair, good, and just, we probably will call in the same energy.

In fact, I just got off a call with a client who told me, "The holidays are coming up, and it's our busiest time of year. It's stressful and never pleasant."

I listened and then said, "But you can change that energy. You can change your relationship with the holidays because your energy is being exchanged every day."

My question for you is, where is your energy being exchanged? Where are you showing up in your life with the same core imprint story? Where is your bottomless negotiation with energy? Where are you negotiating your energetic connection with the world? It may be a story like my client's: the holidays are stressful. Well, you've just negotiated with your energy and pretty much guaranteed that your holidays are going to be stressful.

I recommend flipping this and saying that the holidays are joyful. Identify what you love about the holidays: the lights, the music, the carols, the smell of the air, the joy of making [XYZ]. Whatever it is, focus on and lean into that.

The law of energy means there isn't an area of your life that this doesn't touch. And the nature of energy is that it's in constant motion and influences our thoughts and intentions. Our energy starts with a feeling or situation; we have a thought about it, and then we speak that thought into existence.

So, whatever you may be running from energetically is going to be chasing you. There is no spiritual bypassing with energy. Energy does not lie.

Energy always tells the truth. You can't bend or reshape energy. It is what it is. What you can do, and I can't emphasize this enough, is change your relationship to the situation.

The law of energy intertwines with everything. It's the thread that goes through all the other laws and can work for you. Think of it as the momentum, the wind beneath your wings. And it's so important for you to reset your intentions in guiding your energy.

You're not free-falling through this life. You're not a victim. It is not happenstance. The universe is not random.

Everything is deliberate. Your energy, every day that you show up, is deliberate. Everything you choose is a choice. Everything you connect to is an energetic connection, and you have designed all of it.

I came into the world knowing that I needed to survive. As a five-year-old, I didn't know this, but I was going to attract what I needed, and that was safety. I showed up in the world looking externally for safety, only to discover much later in life that safety lived within me. Energetically, I had to change my connection to safety.

When I realized that safety didn't live in a home, a place, or a person outside of me, that it lived within me, I had to use the law of sacrifice and release what I thought was keeping me safe—my ego energy. The ego will divide, separate, block, and judge, but the heart wants to expand this energy.

You can feel gratitude. You can feel joy. You can also feel fear and hate. Everything is energy, and everything is going to shift your experience and outcome based on the relationship you choose to have with it.

Where are you seeking something, but constantly being disappointed? Perhaps it feels like *Groundhog Day*, where you keep calling in the same thing over and over again.

Working with energy starts within us. The energy that we transmit is what we will attract, and energy influences every aspect of our lives.

There are several misconceptions about energy transformation that can lead to misunderstandings about how energy works and how it can be harnessed in our lives. Some of that might be showing up in your life.

For instance, one of the fundamental principles of physics is that energy cannot be created or destroyed, only transformed. Many people do not fully grasp this, instead believing that energy can simply disappear or appear from out of nowhere. I want you to go back to what I said earlier. Energy is like the wind; it's always present. You have to ask yourself, "Am I allowing my energy to work for me, or is my energy working against me?"

The second misconception is that energy transformation is always positive. The truth is that while energy can be transformed in beneficial ways, it can also manifest as negative energy if it's not consciously directed. For instance, unresolved emotions can cause stress, anxiety, and health problems.

For me, this manifested as migraines. Believe it or not, migraines kept me safe. That's a bold thing to say, but in retrospect, it's exactly what happened. My body shut down, so I found someone to take care of me, and this kept me safe.

The third misconception is that energy transformations happen overnight. Many people expect immediate results from their efforts. I've done this, too: I'm meditating. I'm doing the mantras. What's happening?

In reality, energy transformation is a gradual process that requires consistent effort, intentions, and patience. It's never done. So, set your intention, and you must be consistent with it. If you want your energy to vibrate at a higher level, then you have to look at your life and how you're showing up in it. Are your actions feeding your energy and transmuting what you need out into the world? Once again, it starts with you.

The next misconception involves certain practices that affect energy. Some people believe that only specific spiritual or wellness practices, like meditation, yoga, or religion, can influence their energy. This is not true. Everyday actions, thoughts, and emotions all contribute to the energy transformation. You get to decide what is best for you.

Many people also believe that energy transformation requires special abilities and that you have to be a healer or a shaman to do it. In truth, everyone can influence their energy and transform their experiences through awareness and intention.

The first step in anything, especially energy transformation, is to be aware.

Be aware of the relationships that you're creating. Know that you are the common denominator in your life. You have to ask yourself, "What energy am I transmuting to create this life I'm living?" It's accountability.

Positive thinking alone is not sufficient. You have to maintain a positive mindset, but if you rely on positive thinking without taking action to address the underlying issues, there will be no spiritual transformation. We have to work out our "shizzle" and be truthful with ourselves. Inauthenticity is 1,000% going to lead you to an energetic disconnect with your desires. You must be fearlessly authentic if you want your energy to transform into the truth that you're living.

The next misconception that I want to address is the belief that energy is abstract and unrelated to daily life. In reality, energy transformation is an integral part of our lives.

Every moment, you are being influenced by emotions, relationships, and your overall health and well-being. It is all energy. You are never disconnected from it. If you were disconnected from the energy of life, you would be dead.

This leads to the next misconception: all energy is good energy.

Once again, not all energy is beneficial. Negative energy, such as fear, anger, and resentment, can manifest in harmful ways. Understanding how to recognize and transform negative energy is crucial to personal growth. Ask yourself, "Why am I hurt? Why am I angry?" Usually, underneath that is grief.

The next misconception is that you can control all aspects of your energy. Well, while we have the power to influence our energy, we cannot control every aspect and outcome.

It is crucial to understand that external factors and other people's energy can impact us. You might ask yourself, "Who are the toxic people in my life? Where am I impacted? Where am I influenced? Whose stories am I listening to that I believe to be true about me?" Whatever that story is, it is a lie. You can flip your story and tell your truth, but you must drop into your authentic self. You cannot take on someone else's story about you and live an authentic life.

I want to reinforce the importance of recognizing your worthiness and the power of energy transmutation. Reflect on your experiences with worthiness and energy. Look at where you feel you can transform your life and where the lie lives within you.

Can you use the universal law of sacrifice and make room for the truth? A key factor of the law of perpetual transmutation of energy is that you must show up and own your authentic self. Whether you accept it or not, that connection is what you transmit out into the world. Energetically, anything else will not land correctly.

I want to offer you a few heartfelt and expansive affirmations that you can use to connect with a deeper authenticity within yourself. The law of energy states that it is constantly changing forms. That means that this principle has profound implications for everyday life, including your thoughts, emotions, and actions. What can you do right now to emotionally transform your life? What thought can you implement right now?

Our emotions are energy in motion. When we experience negative feelings like anger and sadness, we consciously choose to transform that energy into something positive, such as something creative or motivational. I want you to engage in activities like exercise, art, and meditation. These can help transform and shift your emotional states.

Next is our mindset and perspective. The way we perceive situations can alter our energy. If 95% of what we hear comes from our subconscious, of which 10% is true and 90% is what we filter through the stories we tell about ourselves, it's easy to see that we can put a negative spin on many things. We can feel helpless.

While having a positive outlook can generate feelings of hope and possibilities, we have to consciously reframe our thoughts. We have to call out the lie: "That is not true. That is not even my story. I don't know where I picked that up."

Maybe we've heard that money doesn't grow on trees. So, we create the lie that money is not available to us. To get money is hard. We're not sure where to find it. We've got a scarcity mindset.

The truth is that we live in a very abundant universe where everything is available. Connecting your energy to abundance puts you on the playing field of unimaginable wealth. And I'm not just talking about money—I'm talking about joy.

All the things that are high or vibrational are available to you, and that shift happens when you decide to call yourself out on the lies. You may even do it aloud: "That's a lie. That's not true."

You might even go a step further and look at when that belief system started. Maybe you were seven when you heard that story. Maybe you were 15 when you realized that you got frightened about something and suddenly scarcity and lack came in. We can create stories, and we pick them up along the way. It is your job to recognize them, find the truth that's anchored in your authenticity, and release the lies.

By consciously reframing our thoughts, we can change the energy we bring into our daily interactions and challenges. Every day, we get to choose how energetically we want to show up and connect, where we're negotiating our energy, and where we are exchanging our energy.

I want to ask you one more time: Where are you showing up and exchanging your energy every day, all day? Unless you're dead, you are energetically exchanging your energy all day long.

The way we perceive situations can alter our energy. A negative mindset makes us feel helpless, while a positive mindset outlook can generate feelings of hope and possibilities. This is why it's important to have clear intentions that direct and transform the energy that we emit into the universe, into the space in front of us, into the person in front of us, into the life we desire.

You are never without tools. You are never helpless. Energy is free. You can create whatever you want, but you must be anchored in your truth, or it will not transmute correctly. It'll be skewed, and you'll have to go back to the drawing board.

When we focus on what we want to attract rather than what we fear or lack, we align our energy with our desires. This is where the universal law of polarity comes in. It's a yin and a yang, and this makes it easier to manifest our goals and our dreams.

Now, unless you're someone who doesn't desire anything and doesn't want more—and I don't believe that to be true, or you wouldn't be here reading this—we all want more of something, and it's going to be found in our energy and what we believe to be true about what we can create.

I think we're all equal on the playing field here. We all can change our energy. What's available to me is available to you.

There is no one-upmanship with energy. No one comes into this world with more energy than anyone else. And the energy we bring into relationships affects their dynamics. Positive energy fosters connections and understanding, while negative energy can create conflict.

How much conflict do you have in your life? How much love do you have in your life? And how much love do you have in your life with underlying conflict that you're afraid to address? By being aware of your energy and choosing to cultivate a supportive and loving environment, you can enhance your interactions with others.

We can build a life of unimaginable expansion, and we can plug anything in there: joy, happiness, gratitude. All these things are high vibrational, energetic movements.

I want to go into something that matters a lot to me right now, and that is energy in our health and well-being. Our physical health is influenced directly by the energy we maintain.

I cannot stress enough that engaging in self-care practices, such as healthy eating, exercise, and mindfulness, can transmute stagnant or negative energy into vitality and well-being. You can flip your life around. I know this to be true.

There is so much shame around this that people tend to stay in the shadows. I have just lost 75 pounds, but I don't want to talk about it because of the shame involved with it.

But the energy I attached was that I wanted to be healthy. I no longer wanted the pendulum to swing back and forth from unhealthy to healthy because it was attached energetically to being skinny. I had to address the shadow work of an eating disorder.

I had to address the trauma in my life. I had to address the generational trauma in my life, and I had to attach it to something as simple as health.

That's what I did. I started walking. I empowered myself to energetically focus on what I could do now.

I could change my mindset. I could attach my thoughts to health. What does that look like? What can I do? I can walk. I can eat healthy.

Once again, I had to use the universal law of sacrifice. I had to give up old thinking and old protective relationships with myself. I had to work through the shame and the energetic vibrational level of what it felt like to stay there.

I can't tell you the joy and peace that comes from working through and sharing where we're at, meeting ourselves there, and paying that forward. That energetic connection is one of resilience and adaptability. This is where energy starts moving.

Life is always going to present challenges and changes, but it also presents rewards that we can't even imagine, because our vibration goes up and we start calling in different levels of energy.

The ability to adapt and transform our responses to these circumstances is crucial. Again, we are never going to raise our energy above where we feel worthy. This is our "high low"; eventually, we have to break through the glass ceiling like Willy Wonka does in his Wonkavator at the end of *Willie Wonka & the Chocolate Factory*. We can change our energy, and this allows us to navigate our lives with grace, resilience, and magic. To continue with the Willie Wonka metaphor—it's our golden ticket.

Always remember that you have the power to transform any experience, every emotion and interaction. By consciously choosing how you direct your energy, you can create a more positive and fulfilling life.

QUESTIONS FOR REFLECTION

Where is your energy being exchanged?

_____

_____

_____

Is your energy working for you or against you?

_____

_____

_____

Are your actions feeding your energy?

_____

_____

_____

What can you do right now to emotionally transform your life?

_____

_____

_____

Where are you showing up and exchanging your energy every day, all day?

_____

_____

_____

CHAPTER 2
YOU'RE NOT ENOUGH (YOU NEVER WILL BE)
THE LAW OF VIBRATION

*"Every thought vibrates. Every thought radiates a signal.
And every thought attracts a matching signal back."*
~ Abraham Hicks

My story was that I was not good enough, and I never would be. That was the vibration I carried. We send our energy out 15 feet in all directions. I can guarantee you that when you meet people, you know how they feel about themselves pretty instantaneously due to this energy field. I learned how to self-sabotage, keeping my vibration where I was familiar.

Believe me when I say we are going to choose the familiar hell over the unfamiliar heaven. It didn't matter what I achieved, and I achieved a lot. I didn't set out to break and set sales records with the United States Chamber of Commerce. I now know that it was trauma-driven. At the time, I had no idea that I was moving so fast, working so hard, and achieving so much. I thought everyone worked at that pace.

I am a competitive person, and I competed against myself the most.

That is where self-sabotage came in. Why would I choose to self-sabotage? And this lasted for years!

When I applied to work with the United States Chamber of Commerce back in the '90s, I showed up where they were interviewing hundreds of people with law degrees, all in suits. I was so intimidated. What if they found out that I had barely graduated from high school? My transcripts had barely caught up with me (as I moved so much).

Evidently, each school's credits are different and with bouncing around so much, I did not have the U.S. history credits that I needed to graduate. My grandmother, being a woman of great influence, met with the superintendents of the district, and let's just say that I got my diploma and walked with my class in the sleepy town on the edge of the wine country in Calistoga, California. Deep inside, it made me wonder if I was smart enough to have a high school diploma.

Back to the interview. I had just had my second child and didn't have a college degree, but I was one of the few candidates selected for a final interview. When they did hire me, they told me I was the black sheep and they would see how it went. The training was intense. I had difficulty memorizing the Senate bills and the relevant legislation, as I knew nothing about politics and didn't even know what a lobbyist was. Remember, it was 1990, so no Google and no cell phones.

Right out of the gate, I set sales records that still haven't been broken. YES, *still* have not been broken. At the end of the day, my feet would be bloody. I'd have to cut my nylons off after walking through industrial parks and gathering support to stop legislation. I believed in what I was doing, and for the first time, I thought that I was connected to very important work. I was one of very few women in my field, and I can guarantee you that the men around me did not embrace me. It was a masculine-dominant industry. I did everything I could to make sure they were comfortable with my success, even to the point of self-sabotaging.

I also suffered an enormous amount of sexual harassment, and I tolerated it. I was terrified. I thought it was acceptable. I thought that if I reported it, I would lose my job. How could I ever land a job with this level of income and prestige again? This opportunity was once-in-a-lifetime. I also believed that I wasn't smart enough to get another one, so I needed to keep quiet and tolerate the harassment. I was once asked to speak at a conference in San Francisco, but when I showed up, there was no conference—just my boss, who was looking for a weekend rendezvous. I went home immediately, but I was devastated.

Then, the migraines came. When I was diagnosed with them, I was 27 and had never had a headache in my life. I went to another professional and then another and another. By that time, I was so sick.

At 28, I had never needed pain medication, not even a Tylenol, even though I had gone through two difficult childbirths with almost 10-pound babies. Now, however, they injected pain and anti-vomiting medicine, and I didn't even know it. All I knew was that I was suffering and wanted it to end. I thought I would die and couldn't function. I had never experienced pain like this before in my life. It was completely debilitating. In fact, the hyperemesis, which is prolonged and uncontrollable vomiting due to mindblowing pain, altered my work schedule and travel. I had no idea how to fix what was happening to me. And the pendulum, again, was swinging. There was no balance.

THE TRUTH: *I was smart enough. I was extraordinarily capable. I was a genius at what I did.*

THE LIE: *I needed a degree like the Scarecrow in Oz to validate my intelligence.*

I had a uniqueness and organic intelligence that always seemed to take me to the top. I was smart enough.

In her book, *Braving the Wilderness*, Brené Brown says, "If you actively seek it, you will always find negativity because you made it your mission. Stop scouring people's faces for evidence that you're not enough." The idea is that actively searching for flaws and negativity ensures that you will find them.

I had no way of embracing my unique way of learning. This lasted for years, and this was a lie. I would attract and build companies, positions, and awards, and sabotage them... because we will never rise above our definition of our worthiness. I was good enough. I was smart enough. I was extraordinarily clever and talented.

Where we vibrate is what we get back. The law of vibration is that everything has a frequency. Even when I was succeeding, my internal frequency was sabotaging me due to the fact that my sense of worthiness couldn't retain that level of success. Believe it or not, this was my comfort zone.

I will add that, even when I started to feel powerful and embrace my success, this particular story stayed with me for years. At a family dinner, I was sharing a record I had just set, and my brother-in-law was aware of some of the executives that I had met with. He chose to tell me that the reason I was successful was because of how I looked... that I was selling sex.

Mind you... I wore conservative suits with white blouses and brooches at the time. The sad part is that it reinforced the part of me that still believed I wasn't smart enough to achieve what I was doing.

How many of you self-sabotage? Our thoughts, emotions, and beliefs vibrate at specific frequencies and influence what we attract. I can't emphasize enough that you can only receive what aligns with your vibration, and I want to highlight the importance of being in alignment with your desire.

I never really desired to work for a lobbyist company and set records, so it makes sense that I would sabotage that. I didn't want it. I needed to make money. I wasn't aligned at all. I never asked myself what I wanted or what I needed, and I certainly wasn't aware of where I was vibrating.

That wasn't even relevant in my life. Survival and safety were relevant, so I took a job that people thought was remarkable. That covered up all my insecurities; I self-protected with a big-ass job title, all the while attracting chaos. I felt not only like a failure but also like a fraud. I did not have a law degree. I wanted one, but this secretly supported my belief system—the "I'm not smart enough" syndrome.

How many of you have ever felt the vibration and energy of imposter syndrome? The principle of the law of vibration is that everything in the universe is in constant motion and emits a vibration. It emits an energy.

So, everything you speak, everything that influences you, everything you attract into your life, is a vibration. Everything is moving. You speak your life into existence—every bit of it. Change your thoughts; change your life. I'm living proof of that.

You can only receive where you're vibrating at. This is why it's so important to know what your desires are and to be aligned with them. I often ask my clients, "What do you desire?" Usually, they don't know. They've created a life out of a vibration, out of a trauma, out of a fear, out of something they heard, a story in their life that doesn't align with their energy.

They may say, "I've always wanted to be an artist," but they were told early on, "You can't be an artist. Artists don't make any money."

Sometimes, we don't have a choice in how we show up in the world. What's stopping you now from claiming what it is you want? If you connect your energy to that vibration, it's almost unstoppable.

How we vibrate in our daily lives is crucial. There are no exceptions to this rule. It applies to every aspect of our lives. Anything you attract is a manifestation of your vibrational state. That means that if you believe it to be true, you're going to vibrate and emit that truth. If you don't believe it's going to be true, it's not going to happen.

Thoughts shape reality. Positive thinking can attract a positive outcome, while negative thinking can lead to a negative experience. If I believe that I'm going to get sick every three days because that's what the world and history have shown me, guess what I'm going to call in? I've programmed my body to get sick every three days.

Now, did I manifest that? It is real. It isn't imaginary. Is vibration imaginary? Is energy imaginary? We can't see it. This is where we have to trust the process. This is where we have to have faith in the positive outcomes that our mind can create. It is more powerful than we can comprehend. We have the power to vibrate and emit energy to call in everything and anything we want.

The truth and empowerment in this is that if we share our story, we're authentic. If our story is authentic, it will vibrate in truth, and that will expand. However, if the ego comes in, it wants to protect the pain around our story. Maybe the world thinks we're successful, but we have imposter syndrome. We don't believe it. There's a disconnect in the truth. They feel the vibration. We feel the vibration.

What I really love to practice here is using affirmations to reinforce my power. I am capable. I am successful. I know how to identify the lie and where my triggers are. I recognize the power of vibration. Take ownership.

Is there anything in your life that stops you from taking ownership of your vibration, your truth, and your energy? Are you powerless in how you show up in the world? Can you change anything at any point in your life right now?

We often stop ourselves because the story is so embedded in our subconscious that we don't believe that we can make a difference, so our vibrational energy gets stuck in an infinite loop. We come to believe it will never change, and then we adapt to and accept our vibration.

I'm here to challenge that.

You can embrace change by understanding that it is a natural part of life that can lead to higher vibrations. Again, this is not a one-and-done. If this resonates with you, if there's an area in your life that you can shift up and change, if there's an area that you think about emotionally and it doesn't feel good, you can start there.

You have different energies in your body. Where do you feel you're vibrating every day? Do you feel it in your solar plexus or your stomach? Do you feel it in your heart energy? Do you feel it in your throat chakra? Do you feel it in your higher sense? Do you feel it in your grounding? There are reinforcements that you can use to release that vibrational energy and reset. It doesn't have to be difficult, and it doesn't have to be expensive, but you do have to choose, and your greatest power in this life is the right to choose. No one can decide for you, so choose empowering thoughts and embrace the change. Understand that change is a natural part of your life and leads to higher vibrations.

Come up with some thought-provoking questions that you can ask yourself. When you vibrate at a different level, you start asking different questions. If you want a different response, you must ask a better question, and if you are vibrating at a different level, your questions will rise to meet you where you are. Understanding this means that you have to identify the lies in your life.

So, ask yourself, "What needs to change? What am I willing to do? What can I release? What have I tolerated? What is unbearable? Where is my heart breaking? Where is the grief? Where is the joy? Where is the happiness?" Look at those vibrational questions and ask yourself, "Where am I in that? You have to identify the lie that is showing up.

When we meet people on the street, we ask them, "How are you today?"

"I'm fine," they say, but their life is a catastrophe. It's not fine, and we vibrationally know that what they're saying isn't true.

What would it take to ask a different question? "Hey, I see you're off today. Is there anything you want to talk about?" To connect on a vibrational level where we're at the truth, we must ask better questions.

First, you need to identify the lies in your life. Where do you think you're hiding in your life? What is the most dominant thought in your life? Maybe you wake up every day and say, "I hate my job. I hate the world. I hate politics." By doing that, you are setting your vibrational tone for the day.

Here's how to flip that. Every morning, my alarm goes off at 3:00 a.m. I love it. I love embracing my day. I'm never tired of showing up aligned and authentic. I was always exhausted when I was seeking answers outside of myself.

I can't say I'm never tired, but I never set the snooze. I get up. I make my coffee. I'm ready. I'm so excited for my day.

I get to work with people, and I get to hear their stories, help them set intentions, and build out a blueprint for their lives. I get to pay it forward, and my vibration is so high because I'm so grateful that I don't wake up with a migraine anymore. The first thing I say is, "I am so grateful that I am well. I am so grateful that I'm healthy. I am so grateful for this life."

The most powerful thing you can do every day is wake up and review three things that you are grateful for. This practice has changed my life. Whereas I used to wake up with fear and anxiety, this practice elevates my vibration for the day.

I say, "All is well in my world. The universe is working for me, not against me. I am safe, I am loved, and I am protected."

Throughout the day, if I am attracting situations that don't align with my desires or feel chaotic and if people are being disruptive, I release them by saying, "God bless their soul. God bless their soul." Then I visualize them in a golden bubble that floats away. What I am doing is meeting a low vibrational situation with a high vibrational tool, and this shift works EVERY TIME.

I start the day off at a high vibrational level, and it sets the tone for my day. How is your day starting? Where do you set your tone? What frightens you the most? I can guarantee you that your most dominant thought is what frightens you, and you may not even realize what your biggest fear is.

My biggest fear was safety, so when it came to money, I would become extremely reactive and incredibly triggered. I would stick my head in the sand. I wouldn't learn more about it because I told myself that I wasn't smart enough.

This vibrational lie created the synergy in my life. It was my biggest, deepest shame. I'm very good with money. I make a lot of money. I am smart. I have rebooted, and anytime this lie shows up, anytime the past shows up to tell me this is who I am, I smile and say, "Oh, no. I understand your relationship to that."

It may be an old part of myself that might be frightened again, and I might show it the safety, the wisdom, the truth, which is: "This is where we are in our life now. There's no reason to be frightened anymore. You are safe. I created safety for us. Do you trust me?"

Trust is a high vibrational energy, and so many times, we do not trust ourselves to make decisions. We second-guess. As an intuitive, I made a lot of bad decisions in my life, but instead of denying it, I own it. I made bad decisions. I second-guessed everything.

Why? Because I didn't own who I was. I was frightened that if I said I was intuitive, I would be judged. More shame. More low vibrational energy, and there's the loop. I had to break the cycle and take ownership. The minute I did, high vibrational energy not only came in, but every day, I set the tone.

Every day, I show my gratitude. I engage in high-vibrational activities. I meditate on my clients. I align, and I call in people who are aligned to work with me. There is nothing random in this universe. Nothing comes into our life that is a coincidence. Everything is deliberate. Everything is working for us or against us, and I believe the universe is working for us. I believe that God wants everything for us.

Now, if I had vibrationally kept the old story going, I would have stayed in victimhood. Everyone steals everything from me. Everyone has betrayed me. There is no love in the world. Why is this happening to me? Instead, I went in and healed this dysregulation.

I found the core wound, the core fear. That's where it starts. We must identify the lies in our lives. Where are you hiding in your life? What is your most dominant thought? What frightens you the most?

I want to encourage you to be truthful. This is your relationship with you. You don't have to share anything with the world. It starts with you, and it ends with you. I want to inspire you to embrace the law of vibration as a tool for transformation and empowerment—and it's free to use every day. I want to invite you to engage with the vibration that is in alignment with the outcome that you wish for right now. What do you want to create? What vibration would create that for you?

Now I'm going to go into some misconceptions about the law of vibration because I think they are important to identify. If you are confused about where this law can be effective and harnessed in your life, let's go over a few areas that might clarify this.

The first misconception is that vibration is just about positive thinking. Many people believe that simply thinking positively will raise their vibration. Not true. While positive thinking is so important, the law of vibration encompasses a broader range of emotions, beliefs, and actions. It is always anchored in the action. If your actions are doing one thing and your thoughts are doing another, you are not aligned with your truth.

It's essential to address underlying issues and emotions to create lasting change. This is not a one-and-done. In her book, *Mirror Work*, Louise Hay recommends 21 days of mirror work to change your thought process.

If we are committed to this, if we want it, it isn't enough to look in the mirror and say, "I love me," if we don't believe it to be true. It is so important that we understand that to create lasting change, we must address our true belief systems about ourselves.

Another misconception is that all vibrations are equal. All vibrational frequencies are indeed equally effective. However, certain vibrations, such as love, joy, and gratitude, resonate at a higher frequency and attract more positive experiences, while lower vibrations, like anger, fear, and resentment, can attract negative experiences.

This can be a cycle that we create. I wake up with gratitude. I implement high vibrational practices, and because of that, my days are high vibrational.

This does not mean that bad things don't happen. It just means that when they do, I step back and say, "Isn't that interesting? How can this work for me? What do I need to know? How can my vibrational energy align with what the answer is? What is the resolution? What do I need to know from this energy coming at me? Because this is my solution.

The next misconception is that vibration is a one-and-done change. Some people believe that you can raise your vibration once and maintain it without any further effort. I'm going to say again that vibrational states require ongoing awareness, intention, and repetition.

Life circumstances, emotions, and thoughts can fluctuate. Most people live in their past experiences. They jump over the present moment, where all their power is, and jump into the future of the "what if." We have no power there. Life fluctuates.

Anything can happen. If we think we're in control, we're not. What we can control is how adaptable we are and what questions we can ask. There is no one-and-done here. It is about raising our vibration to address the situation, and it requires us to, again, ask better questions.

Another misconception is that we can control everything we attract. While we can influence our vibration and attract certain experiences, it is truly a misconception that we have complete control over every aspect of our lives. External factors and the vibrations of others play a significant role here.

We are impacted by the level at which we accept people's negative vibrations and take ownership of them. When we take someone else's story on, we take on their vibration and their ideas.

The next misconception is that vibrations are only about emotions. While emotions are a significant part of vibrations, they also include thoughts, beliefs, and actions. I'm going to say that again. Thoughts, beliefs, and actions are all connected.

All of these elements contribute to your overall vibrational frequency and affect what you attract into your life. If you want to change your mindset and thoughts, but you decide not to take action or change your belief system, the whole system is going to fall apart. It's not sustainable. You cannot lie about energy. Energy is energy is energy. Vibration supports energy. Your vibration is your energy, and they go hand in hand. All the elements will support or not support your life.

Another misconception is that raising your vibration means ignoring negative emotions. No, never, absolutely not. However, acknowledging and processing these emotions is crucial for true healing and transformation, ultimately leading to a more authentic and higher vibrational state. You will not do that. You will be anchored in what it is you are not willing to address, and that is where you will vibrate.

I ask again: What do you not want to feel? We must feel it all. There is a popular saying: "You must feel it to heal it." That is relevant here.

One common misconception is that the law of vibration is separate from other universal laws. I hear this a lot, and this is surprising to me because many people view the law of vibration as an isolated principle when, in reality, it is deeply interconnected with the other universal laws.

Understanding these relationships will only enhance your understanding of energy, how vibration operates, and how you can use it in your life. The most important thing here is to understand that you are energy, that you vibrate at a certain level, and that your story creates what you emit into the world and what you receive.

Another misconception is that we must be perfect to attract good things. This is a lie. In truth, everyone has fluctuations in their vibrations. We have good and bad days. As it says in the Four Agreements, we must always do our best. Raising our vibration doesn't always happen, but if we want to attract a higher vibration, we do not need to achieve a state of perfection. Perfection does not exist.

Every time you want to be perfect, you abandon ship. You abandon yourself. Use the universal law of sacrifice and give up perfection because perfection paralysis is real. It will keep you locked into a cycle where you will never vibrate and attract what you want.

That leads me to vibration as a mystical concept. Many people dismiss the law of vibration as a mystical, esoteric idea, believing it lacks any scientific backing. However, the principles of vibration are supported by quantum physics and psychology, and the real-world implications of vibrational states are demonstrable. Many people think that vibrations are fixed and unchangeable. In fact, they are dynamic and can shift rapidly based on thoughts, emotions, and experiences.

Recognize that fluidity empowers people to take control of their vibrational states. It always astonishes me when people decide that they are energy and control their vibrations. I have witnessed miracles happen in people's lives. I have watched their vibrational states and lives change, and it still makes my chest vibrate at how beautiful it is to watch them harness the enormous power that they hold. By addressing misconceptions, you can develop a nuanced understanding of the law of vibration, how it works effectively, and how effectively you can apply its principles to create the changes you want in your life.

There are several activities and practices that I like to do that will help raise your vibration. If you can incorporate these into your daily routine, it will lead to a more positive and fulfilling life. Isn't that what we're here for? Is there anyone who says they want a dark life filled with drama and filled with chaos? Your life might reflect that, but you don't desire it. You may not think you can change it, but I'm here to tell you that you can.

Regular meditation can lead to increased awareness, inner peace, and heightened vibrational states. You might think that you cannot meditate, but I guarantee that I can find a zillion ways to find a state of meditation that works for you. For example, go outside, place the palm of your hand, which connects to your heart energy, on a tree, and take some deep breaths. You're meditating.

Do not overthink the state of meditation. You do not have to be in a "kumbaya" state of deep meditation to get benefits. Meditation is quieting the mind. Start there. Use what you have.

Next, embrace gratitude. Not everybody's a writer. Not everybody wants to keep a gratitude journal. However, writing is secondary; saying you're grateful aloud is a beautiful practice. Writing it down and using positive affirmations daily can help reprogram your limited beliefs and create a higher vibration. Use phrases like "I am worthy," "I attract positivity," "I am capable of achieving my dreams and can be incredibly powerful." Do not minimize the power of words. If you want to raise your vibration, you must create a new language.

But don't neglect physical activity. Engage in regular exercise, whether it's yoga, dance, or walking. I love to walk, and it connects me with nature. Any preferred activity releases endorphins and boosts your mood. Isn't that what we're looking for? A higher level of vibration?

Physical movement clears stagnant energy from the body and elevates your vibrational frequency. I clap my hands in the daytime because it shakes up my arms, hits my heart, releases my chakras, and energizes me.

There are many easy, simple ways to reset. Spending time in nature is one of the things I desire most. It is incredibly grounding and uplifting, whether it's a walk in the park, a hike in the mountains, or simply sitting outside. Nature can help raise your vibe and connect you with the earth. There's something called "earthing," where you take your shoes off and connect your feet with the vibration of the earth. It is scientifically proven to raise your vibration and reset your energy. It's not a one-and-done, but if you do this, you will see a change in a very short period.

Nutrition is also important: eating a balance of rich, whole foods, fruits, and vegetables and cutting out processed food. Nutritious foods can positively affect your energy levels and vibrational state. Far too many times, I have heard from a client, "I went out drinking last night and feel terrible. It's ruined my whole day. My vibrations have been low and off all day. I've also been eating lots of sugar."

Sugar causes inflammation of the brain and body. It doesn't make us feel good. Drink water. Nothing can reset our body more than staying hydrated. Keeping our brains hydrated has been scientifically proven to raise our vibrations.

Practice consciously breathing. I love "box breath." It's so easy. One, two, three, four in—one, two, three, four out. It doesn't have to be difficult. Breathwork can lead to a sense of calm and clarity and a high vibrational state. And we can take breathwork all the way into releasing deep trauma into the body.

Use intention when you breathe: What do you want to release from your body? Use everything to vibrationally work for you.

Surround yourself with positive energy and engage with uplifting people. They say the five people we surround ourselves with set our vibrational level. Who are you being influenced by? Who are you spending your time with? Are they tearing you down on a daily basis? Are they uplifting you? Are they supporting you? Pay close attention to who you're spending time with.

Engage in creative activities: painting, writing, playing music. This is an incredibly powerful way to raise your vibrational state. I don't paint or draw, but I can doodle. I don't shame myself for not being able to do any of those talented things.

I can't even yodel. I sing terribly, but it doesn't stop me from singing. Sometimes, I even put it out there in my Instagram stories.

"Laughter yoga" is another great activity. It's an exercise where, all of a sudden, you're laughing so hard that it releases your vibrational state. I listened to myself. You don't even need to hear anything funny. It just changes the vibrational energy of your body.

Acts of kindness create a ripple effect of positive energy. Being of service not only raises your vibration but also contributes to a sense of connection and purpose. Get outside of yourself. It's not all about you.

Your vibration affects everything. Think about the billions of people in the world. We are all connected vibrationally and energetically. What we do and say matters. Being present and practicing mindfulness can reduce your anxiety and increase awareness of your thoughts and emotions. This intentional shift changes your vibrational state.

"Sound healing," like singing bowls, tuning forks, and listening to high-frequency music, can help evolve your vibration. Sound has a profound effect on our energy and can promote healing and relaxation.

How many times have you left a concert and you're so jacked up because of the vibrational energy of the show? Same thing.

You can do this without spending. I don't know how much a ticket to a concert is now. Well, I just went to Lady Gaga, and I think I paid

$1,100 for my ticket. It was worth it. The energy around me, the singing, being close to the state—it was everything I needed.

Anytime I want to tap into that high vibrational energy, all I have to do is listen to one of my videos. I can feel the energy of the people around me. That's vibrational energy. Visualize what you want. Identify the emotions associated with what you wish to attract. This practice will help your thoughts become a reality.

Creating a clean and organized environment can also positively impact your energy. When you have a cluttered space, you can feel stagnant. Decluttering can create a more harmonious living space and allow more freedom—freedom of movement, freedom of thought, freedom of space, and freedom of vibrational energy.

Limiting negative media consumption, including social media and the news, can help protect your energy, too. If you don't think that such exposure can lead to negative energy, I'm here to tell you that it can and will. If you want your vibrational energy to be higher, connect with a source that aligns with your desires.

By incorporating everything that we have said above, not only can you raise your vibration, but it can lead to a more positive mindset. It can lead to better physical and emotional health and a greater ability to attract what you desire. This is the law of desire, which we'll be talking about soon, but the key is consistency here and finding what resonates best with you.

Personally, this is not one size fits all. Everyone connects differently. Everybody desires something different. What is it you desire? What do you want? Where are you showing up? Where are you connecting? Where are you of service? This matters. The law of vibration is how we communicate with the world. Where are you communicating? Is that enough?

To wrap this up, I want you to remember that everywhere you vibrate, you activate, and everywhere you activate, you vibrate.

QUESTIONS FOR REFLECTION

What is the most dominant thought in your life?

_____

_____

_____

What do you want to create?

_____

_____

_____

What do you not want to feel?

_____

_____

_____

Who are you being influenced by, and are they tearing you down or supporting you?

_____

_____

_____

What is it you desire?

_____

_____

_____

Where are you showing up?

_____

_____

_____

CHAPTER 3
EVERYTHING IS CONNECTED
THE LAW OF ABUNDANCE

"The Lord God made the earth and the heavens and every plant of the field before it was in the earth, and every herb of the field before it grew."
~ Genesis 2:4–5

Everything is already available to you, and you already have the answers. As Abraham Hicks said, "The universe is abundant with everything that you want. Nothing is lacking. It is not testing you. It's benevolently providing for you."

I left Calistoga when I turned 17. I had just graduated high school and wanted to go to college. I thought I had a trust fund set up, but I discovered that I didn't. I lived in a world where lots was promised that gave me a false sense of security and nothing was followed through.

I had no idea where I was going

Let me add that it was a peaceful day, nothing out of the ordinary... The reason I left was as simple as this: my grandmother had fulfilled her job. I had graduated, so her responsibilities were over.

I was abandoned again, thrown out into the world with no guidance, connection, or safety, just me and two garbage bags full of clothes. I had no cell phone, no Google Maps, just AC/DC, Peter Frampton live, and *The Best of Bread* on eight-track.

Racing down the highway with my windows down and music blasting, I cried all the way to Santa Rosa, wondering if anyone would ever want me. I had no idea where I was going. I would've been the perfect kidnapping victim because it would've been months before anyone realized I was missing. During this period of my life, I was a nomad. I desperately wanted the life I envisioned—earning a law degree, getting married, because to me it meant safety—but I was living from couch to couch and in survival mode, looking for jobs with no qualifications and being put in some pretty horrific and compromising situations.

What was abundant about my universe? At every turn, I was hopeful. Regardless of my circumstances, I believed that the world was a good place. I found joy in the little things. When I got 15 cents, I would go to Thrifty and get a three-decker ice cream cone, and you would've thought I'd won the lottery.

I spent an enormous amount of time alone, as people frightened me. It was the '80s; there were a lot of parties, a lot of cocaine, a lot of everything, and I was a very naïve, fear-filled young girl. I said no to everything—safety was all that I focused on.

I think it was difficult for the world—and for me, too—to realize that while I looked like I came from extreme wealth, lack and scarcity were embedded in me, as was the fear of abandonment. This mindset didn't allow me any abundance—or the idea that abundance even existed.

It would be impossible to explain all the trauma that unfolded over the next few years.

THE TRUTH WITHIN THE LIE

THE LIE: *I was not loved. I was not wanted. I had no value in the world or to myself. I was desperately seeking to belong somewhere.*

THE TRUTH: *I was worthy of being loved, and I did belong. I found out years later that the home I was searching for lived in me. I can honestly say now that it is a beautiful place to come home to.*

As I grew older, I recognized that no matter what money I seemingly came from, the stories that I came from were of the mindset of scarcity. I came out of a home where I heard on the daily, "Money doesn't grow on trees, young lady," and "You have to work hard for what you want."

This led me to believe that abundance was limited, creating a disconnect between my vibrational childhood dreams and the world's constraints. I began to doubt my worthiness and ability to attract what I desired.

Not only did I not believe that money grew on trees, but I also truly believed you had to work hard for what you wanted. We have to take action, but this does not connect with the law of abundance. This erroneous belief made me overwork and prevented the law of abundance from coming into play.

That internal shift caused a rift in my self-esteem and my connection with the universe. I moved from a state of openheartedness to one of guardedness, where fear and self-doubt dictated my actions. I started to measure my worth by external achievements and material possessions, losing sight of abundance and what existed around and within me.

I want you to know that abundance is not just about material wealth; it's about recognizing the richness of experience, relationships, and opportunities and allowing that to expand. You can only access that in your present moment, so if you want a more abundant life, you have to develop a practice that you become anchored to.

You can only anchor in the present moment. If you're anchored in the past, you're forever second-guessing yourself. If you're anchored in the future, you're always what-if-ing yourself because you have no power in either the past or the future. Your power in abundance is cultivated in the here and now.

I really love to gratitude journal, which is just to take a few moments to write down a few things I'm grateful for. Don't generalize; really feel what you're grateful for because this practice shifts the focus from lack to the abundance that exists in your life.

This is how I did it in my life. I recognized that true abundance already existed. Abundance never abandoned me. I abandoned my relationship with abundance because of fear. What keeps us in the grind? Fear, doubt, worry. At an early age, I took these on, and abundance was no longer available to me.

Another tool you can use to recognize abundance is affirmations. Create a set of affirmations that resonate deeply with yourself: "I attract abundance effortlessly. I am open to receiving all the good things that the universe has to offer." Affirmations like these serve as powerful reminders of your inherent worthiness.

Believe it or not, when we get a jolt, we often no longer believe that things are available to us. This is why the subconscious is so powerful. It tries to protect us, saying, "You might have been happy, but it wasn't safe. Look what happened."

We think, *"Oh, right, that wasn't safe. I need to protect myself."* Then, we cut off our ability to expand in this unbelievably abundant universe.

The third tool is visualization. Each night, I spend a few minutes visualizing my goals and desires as if I've already achieved them. I call this my higher self. I immerse myself in the feelings of joy and fulfillment that come from achieving these things.

It's kind of like when I speak on stage. I do not visualize how frightened I am or what I need to remember. Instead, I think about the happiest times of my life, the most connected, grounded, and joyful moments. It has nothing to do with what I'm going to talk about, but it brings in the abundance and the expansion of my body. I immerse myself in that.

I can't stress enough how important visualization is to achieving what you desire. This practice aligns your energy with the abundance you wish to attract.

The fourth tool is mindfulness and meditation. Now, you might see this repeated with every law, and the reason for this is that it works. These moments of stillness allow us to connect with our inner selves and the universe, reminding us that abundance flows naturally when we're present and aware.

Next, I want you to recognize what disrupts your flow of abundance because it's important to identify the thoughts and behaviors that can throw you out of alignment.

We've discussed how 95% of the stories we tell ourselves come from the subconscious. A lot of that is negative self-talk we're not even aware of. That's why it's called the subconscious.

Whenever I notice a critical voice in my head saying I'm not enough or I'll never get what I want, I consciously challenge that thought and replace it with a more empowering belief. Sometimes, I get angry and say, "That is not true. It's an old story, and I'm not going to tolerate it anymore."

You get to choose your relationship with these thoughts and beliefs. I have learned that comparing myself to others diminishes my sense of abundance. Nothing can spiral me faster into feeling that I'm not good enough than comparing myself to someone else's journey, so I focus intensely on my unique journey and celebrate my wins, no matter how small.

I'm going to say it again: *Celebrate your wins, no matter how small.* If you constantly compare yourself to others and do not acknowledge what you've done, you cannot expand the abundance in your life.

Next, I remind myself that failure is often a stepping stone to success. It is essential to our expansion and learning curve. Embracing the lessons learned from setbacks helps us maintain a positive outlook on our journeys. We must ask ourselves, "What do I need to know from this? What do I need to learn?" Boom, we're expanding our knowledge and abundance of what we desire from the universe.

When I reflect on my journey, I realize that the universe is not only abundant, but we are all deserving of its gifts. By shifting our mindsets, employing daily practices, and recognizing the barriers that hinder our flow of abundance, we can begin to cultivate a rich life filled with joy, grace, love, and high vibrational feelings.

So, I invite you right now, my dear readers, to join me in rediscovering the abundance that awaits you in this vast universe. Together, we're going to break free from the limiting beliefs and embrace the limitless possibilities that are rightfully ours. It is our birthright to claim this abundance.

I want you to look at your foundational belief system and your relationship to abundance. Where did your relationship with it become guarded? Perhaps it no longer felt safe to live in such an expansive world.

This is where the abundant mindset is limitless. If you are limiting yourself on a daily basis because of a scarcity mindset, I'm here to tell you that what you believe is what you receive.

I'm going to say that again: what you believe is what you receive. The law of attraction works in relation to abundance, so if I believe that I'm going to get a cinnamon lollipop every day, my abundant universe is satisfied. It doesn't have to be quantum leaping here. It just means that what you desire is available to you. I want to emphasize the importance of aligning your thoughts and feelings with abundance.

We have to identify the limiting beliefs we hold about abundance, like "I don't deserve it" and "There's not enough for everyone." If such beliefs don't live within you, I tip my hat to you. You have not only claimed abundance, but you live in an abundant universe.

However, most of us struggle with our belief system, and our minds can't expand to embrace what is available to us according to the universal law of abundance.

I want you to revisit your goals and dreams without any restrictions, without any narrative, without any "coulda, woulda, or shoulda." Are you living the life of abundance that you could be living?

Do what you can do to change your belief system: gratitude journaling, affirmations, and visualizations. And remember, the importance of surrounding yourself with positive influences and experiences is exponential. I can't stress enough that the people you call in will support your mindset.

What we ground into is our "I am." If we ground into abundance, what would that feel like? What would we say about ourselves each day?

"I am abundant. I am full of wealth. I am joyful. I am grateful."

But if we say these things, are we taking action to support them? Does our life reflect this?

I want you to look at where you have grounded yourself and what you think is available to you. Then, write out a personal experience of what abundance feels like. Even during challenging times, even when you're frightened, do you push through and say, "I know an abundant world is still available to me"? Or do you adapt to the external world around you and limit yourself? When you affirm your existence, you claim, "I am abundant," shifting the energy of your life.

I also want you to connect with your sense of worthiness. Tell yourself, "I am worthy of living an abundant life regardless of my circumstances, regardless of what's happened in my life, regardless of the stories I've told myself. At this moment, I can claim something." This plants a spiritual seed that expands.

It is never too late. You are never too old to activate the law of abundance. The journey toward abundance is about your limited beliefs and believing in the expansion that you can step into.

The sky's the limit, but do you believe this when you say it? Your call to action here is to step toward embracing abundance in all areas of your life. I want you to do a 180 in your life.

I want you to revisit all areas of your life. For each, ask yourself, "Does it exhibit abundance? Does it scream lack, scarcity, and fear? Are my decisions coming from a place of love or a place of fear?" The answers to those questions will decide how much abundance you receive in your life.

The law of abundance is available to everyone. It's available to you if you believe it. The only limits to the abundance you receive are the ones you place on yourself. This is how your self-imposed limiting beliefs hinder your abundance.

The opposite is true as well. For example, say I want to make a million dollars by the end of the year. I can write out a blank check for a million dollars and put it in a drawer. By doing that, I have activated the law of abundance and planted a seed of expansion.

What seeds of expansion are you planting? I love the analogy of gardening because I love watching things grow. I love planting seeds. I know they need to be nurtured. I know they need to be cared for, just like the law of abundance, just like our dreams, our belief systems. We nurture everything into existence and give signals to the universe when we're ready to receive.

People often struggle with this because the mindset flip requires us to fully embrace abundance. If we want something but our belief system tells us something else, are we going to receive it? By acknowledging what your belief system is, we can engage in this law and claim what we want.

It's also crucial to realize that your belief systems around this law may stem from narratives that are not even yours. The truth about abundance is that it is unlimited. It's not just for the lucky or chosen few. Success is available to all of us.

People often mistakenly believe that poverty is inescapable. They've been poor for generations, and there's no way out. That is a limiting belief. Yes, life has given them fewer tools and opportunities, but with an abundant mindset, you attract opportunities. You call in and reinforce your abundance of what you want.

Now, this is not a one-and-done. We not only must anchor into it and focus on it, but we must also take action and challenge the scarcity narratives. We must challenge our belief systems.

I encourage you to focus on the affirmations of love, joy, wealth, health, and friendship with abundance. Gossiping about friends isn't going to be expansive. That's not going to activate the law of abundance in your life.

Look at the relationships in all aspects of your life: the love in your life, the friendships in your life, the partnerships in your life, perhaps your marriage, your work life, where you dream. Do you activate the law of abundance? Or do you think that it's just for the lucky few who seem to be blessed with wealth, love, and opportunities?

As author and motivational speaker Wayne Dyer said, "Abundance is not something we acquire. It's something we tune into." And the frequency we tune into is a vibration.

We're activating a law of vibration here. Introducing the law of abundance governs the flow of resources, relationships, and opportunities in your life. So, if you want your story to follow, you must cultivate an abundant mindset.

As a child, my abundant universe was the feeling I got of safety, love, and consistency. I created the world I needed, to feel abundant. I can still hear the laughter echoing in the air and smell the grass under my feet. I can see the floral dress I'm wearing, and I can feel my dad's energy.

My dad drowned when I was 30 years old, so I no longer have him in the physical realm of this world, but I can guarantee you that in the spiritual world, my dad showed up abundantly to guide me.

My dad's daily ritual of giving me the cinnamon lollipop made me feel cherished and abundant. What stories have you created in your world that feel abundant? It doesn't have to matter to anyone else, but it has to matter to you.

Nobody has your unique story. Your turning point will be when you identify the moment you stopped believing that the law of abundance was available to you and started putting parameters and stories around it.

We can live in the two conflicting worlds of scarcity and abundance. We can hold space for both. We do not spiritually bypass what happens in our lives, but we have to realize that our relationships to what is available to us change according to universal laws.

You need to claim abundance and write it down. Then you will be what you decide you will be. Recognizing this law means not only claiming it but also visualizing that it's already done. It's not a one-and-done.

You're not seeking abundance, and you're not finding it. You are just in your higher self, claiming it and moving in that direction.

Daily mantras, story changes, and gratitude keep you at a vibrational level where you can activate the universal law of vibration and send the signals to the universe that you are willing and ready to receive. Our beliefs are key here. You must believe that you can access the abundance.

Re-examine how you've shaped your reality and where you find yourself today. Look at the importance of the law of abundance and understand why you may struggle with it. Is it your story, or is it someone else's that you picked up?

For me, it was: "You have to work hard, young lady." And guess what? I worked really hard, but I didn't understand that the law of abundance was not available to me because that's not something I associated with working hard. What do you associate the stories in your life with?

Many people struggle with this law due to limiting beliefs and storytelling. If we want to flip it, we have to tell ourselves the truth about abundance, that it's unlimited. Again, we have to challenge our stories. We have to cultivate abundance. We have to encourage ourselves: "I will seek more. I have more. I am more."

We have to emphasize the importance of giving and receiving with a flow of abundance. We must be receiving and giving. There must be a flow with abundance. We have to shift our narrative with this, and we have to practice the applications in our daily lives, such as daily mantras.

We have to say, "I am aware of what I'm choosing. I choose abundance. I choose love. I choose health." Whatever it is we want more of, we must choose it. By doing so, we activate the law of abundance.

I encourage you to confront the limiting beliefs that create lack or even envy. Celebrate successes and foster a sense of community rather than competition because we are living in an abundant universe.

The universe is inherently abundant. It is so abundant that if you put the energy out there and celebrate others, I guarantee you that your tide will rise as well. You'll be internalizing the belief system that you are abundant and living in an abundant universe; that is a beautiful place to start.

What action steps can you take today to get started? What pivotal things can you do today? Look at your current relationships that hold emotions like anger, fear, and grief. These keep you in the grind and in the old stories.

What would it look like if you shifted to an abundant mindset? You would have to use the law of sacrifice and release the anger, fear, and grief. We don't spiritually bypass. We just hold space for both. We know that in an abundant universe, abundant healing is available to us, and we have to claim that.

This is where your abundant potential lives. I want you to look at the fact that your powerful call to action is taking tangible steps toward cultivating an abundant life and recognizing that everything is available to you.

Simply saying, "I'm claiming the law of abundance," will expand your energy and put you on the playing field. But reflecting on your limited beliefs and mindset is essential to cultivating a life of abundance. Shifting your focus, enhancing positivity, reinforcing abundance, improving resilience, attracting more abundance, building stronger relationships, encouraging generosity, cultivating mindsets, reframing your challenges, and creating daily habits are all part of how you do this.

Here are a few tips to help you shift your focus. Gratitude is key. By regularly acknowledging and appreciating the positivity in your life, you can reduce feelings of scarcity and enhance feelings of abundance.

Practicing gratitude increases positive emotions and overall life satisfaction. Who doesn't want to be more satisfied in their life? When we focus on gratitude, we are more likely to experience joy, contentment, and fulfillment; with each essential component of our abundant mindset —boom—it's activated.

Gratitude reinforces the belief that abundance exists in various forms. You can celebrate this through small victories, relationships, and opportunities. For example, when people in the checkout line of the grocery store smile at you, you might say, "Thank you for being such a great part of my day." By doing things like that, you start to see abundance as a constant presence in your life rather than a fleeting experience.

A gratitude practice also enhances emotional resilience. Gratitude is the highest vibrational practice you can use, and it's free. It is available to you every moment of every day. You just have to choose it.

What we focus on expands, and when we're faced with challenges, if we can say, "I'm so grateful for that lesson," it equips us with a more positive outlook to find solutions and reinforce our belief systems and ability to create abundance. Instead of focusing on the difficulties, we focus on the solutions and how grateful we are that the opportunity gave us more abilities for more solutions.

That allows us to attract more abundance because what we focus on expands. Then, by cultivating a mindset of gratitude, we send out positive vibrations that attract more positive experiences and opportunities in our lives. Through gratitude, we can strengthen relationships, fostering connections and trust instead of tearing them down.

Upgrading your words is very important. You might be programmed to show up because you have an old narrative that you just keep repeating. It's just *Groundhog Day*, and you're looping.

So, put yourself in a supportive network that feels abundant, in relationships that feel emotionally supportive, and with resources that are collaborative and full of growth. Seek them out. As the Sufi poet, Rumi, said, "What we're seeking is seeking us."

It's the red car theory—when someone asks you, "Have you seen any red cars?" you may say no. Then, the next day, you spy dozens of red cars. The red car theory suggests that once you start noticing something specific, you start to see it everywhere. This can be applied to all aspects of your life, including your thoughts. I believe that energetically.

Cultivating a mindset from this means practicing gratitude, encouraging mindfulness, and promoting awareness in the present moment. This is where everything happens.

This awareness is going to help us appreciate our current circumstances, and it reduces anxiety about the future and regrets about the past—which can foster a sense of what? Abundance. If we can reframe challenges as opportunities for growth and learning and recognize the lessons from difficult experiences, the obstacles we face will contribute to our overall journey toward abundance rather than impede us.

Everything in my life has led me to where I am now. If I had done one turn differently, it would not have landed me in the abundant life I claim and live now. Every bit of it, as difficult as it was, as deep and dark as the shadow work was, I'm grateful for it because I want to learn.

I want to know. I want to do better. I must claim that, and this will create a daily habit.

A gratitude practice is a daily habit of creating abundance. If you do this practice regularly, it will reinforce a positive mindset and help you be consistent with your commitment to live an abundant life. I can't stress enough the role that gratitude plays in the law of abundance.

It's fundamental to enhancing positivity, attracting more abundance, and fostering resilience and connection, which is why we are all here. If you decide to incorporate gratitude right now, you can expect to transform your life and create more abundance, not only exponentially but immediately. This is not a one-and-done, but I can guarantee you that you will see things that will make you say, "I can't believe that just happened."

Well, you created it. You created a new story. You created a new energy to show up in.

You created an abundant playing field, and it all starts when you decide that everything's available to you and that the old story is not going to rule the roost anymore. Unlock the cage of false stories, throw away the key, and say, "You know what? I understand that the terror barrier was built from the false stories that I've lived in to keep myself safe. I live in an abundant universe with an unlimited supply of resources and wealth available to me. There are no chosen ones; there are no lucky ones. I am doing things differently."

Do this, and not only will life offer you more, but you will also get to decide whether you become wealthy because the universe is not random. How you practice the law of abundance is important: "I see more; I will have more."

You have to give and receive, and in this repetitiveness, you get to choose to have an abundant or negative relationship with everything in your life. You can sabotage yourself if your beliefs are limiting. Or you can choose to expand in the abundance that you already have.

You will not know what the future holds, and here's a real insight: you never do, but the universe is working for you, not against you. If you are going through a bad experience right now, stop and ask yourself: What are you attracted to? What cycles are you repeating? What traumas are you recreating? I want you to say, "I can shift my belief systems. I'm changing my relationship to the stories that I've lived up to this point."

If you want to be more in your life, you have to choose it. You have to choose more love, joy, wealth, health, and safety. Yes, more safety. My world was shattered, and I have the cinnamon lollipops on my desk today to remind me that safety and abundance live within. I challenge the stories that create lack and scarcity in my life; they still come up, but I challenge them.

I celebrate everyone's wins. There is no competition; there is no envy. We are all connected by abundance. I want everyone to live their lives. My heart expands when I see the success in people's lives.

You get to decide right now: "Am I choosing abundance, or am I choosing an old story that may not even have been mine to begin with?" The lie is the story; the truth is that everything is available to you.

QUESTIONS FOR REFLECTION

Are you living a life of abundance?

_____

_____

_____

What stories have you created in your world that feel abundant?

_____

_____

_____

What do you associate the stories in your life with?

_____

_____

_____

Are you choosing abundance, or are you choosing an old story that may not have been yours to begin with?

_____

_____

_____

What would it look like if you shifted to an abundant mindset?

_____

_____

_____

CHAPTER 4
THE BRUTAL BALANCER
UNIVERSAL LAW OF POLARITY

"Everything is dual; everything has poles; everything has its pair of opposites; like and unlike are the same; opposites are identical in nature, but different in degree."
~ The Kybalion

I was sitting at my desk, getting ready for my five o'clock client, when I got a message from a former client about an article that had been released. It said: "Local practitioner being charged with sexual misconduct."

As I read it, I began to realize that the article was about my husband. I couldn't breathe. I couldn't move. I did not believe it was true. How could it be? He was my rock, the safest person in my life—he was my protector. HE LOVED ME. He would never betray me or our children.

I don't think it's important to dive into the deep details here, but I feel that knowing about it is necessary to understand my evolution. This was the final catalyst to understanding and breaking a trauma bond and trusting at a level where I was freefalling into the universe. I had never been safer in my life.

The universal law of polarity is a universal law that states that everything has an opposite. The law suggests that opposites are two extreme states of the same phenomenon and every experience of the situation contains both sides—for instance, love and hate, joy and sorrow, and success and failure.

But this law emphasizes that these opposites are interconnected and necessary for understanding and living life fully.

So, back to my story. At that moment, the pendulum swung. Love, hate, betrayal—all of it. It's a mixed bag. Eventually, I learned how to hold space for both. The healing process? Well, that would take time.

So, my husband of 25 years ended up forfeiting his medical license and being prosecuted, and the world as I knew it was over. The betrayal that I felt uprooted my sense of security and safety, and I now realized that what I'd thought to be true was a lie and the polar opposite of what I had lived.

I was shattered. That was the moment it all came undone. I needed help, so I chose to work with a trauma therapist, who allowed me to safely unpack it all. The biggest surprise was connected to my core wound, my core story of why I called in so much betrayal in my life.

I grieved, I cried, I healed, and I met myself at a level I didn't know existed. There's no perfect process, no linear line to healing, but I was committed to the conviction that I would never trust someone more than I trusted myself.

The pendulum would continue to swing from one side to the other, and I could hold space for both. I'd never understood the depths of the betrayal I was calling in, but then I realized that this story wasn't just about marriage; it was about my core wound and the world of safety and betrayal from a primary parent that I continued to call in because that was what I knew to be true.

Now, I have healed from that story, and it changed my life, my stability, and my safety. Everything I knew to be true in my world reconnected to a more organic place of universal laws where everything expanded for me. I no longer lived in a world where I second-guessed my truth.

THE LIE: *I exchanged love for safety and forfeited intimacy for what he was able to give, which was acts of service.*

THE TRUTH: *I deserve and am worthy of a deep, intimate love where I wasn't too much. And that would mirror back a deep connection and love to me that I didn't need to negotiate.*

Hardly. It was THE most difficult time as I had to learn how to grieve and hold space for joy, too. He had done terrible things, but I still believed that he was a good man, too. It wasn't one or the other.

You could say that I was living a lie, but I guarantee you that the inner child needed safety and believed she had it with him. She needed it to be true, and that's how I showed up; that's what I honored. At the time, I did not know why that pendulum was swinging. I do know now, and that's why this chapter is so important.

Here's how the law of polarity works. It operates on the premise that for every positive, there is a negative, and vice versa, and this duality is essential for balancing growth. I have come to understand that, had I not experienced this betrayal, I would have continued to call in more betrayals like I had many times in my life.

I learned to drop into abundance and gratitude. At the time, I was not grateful that my heart had been ripped out of my soul, but I am so grateful for that lesson now because I will never call in betrayal again. I am so aware of what it is I'm calling in and who's running the show. I was willing to go behind the terror barrier and dive into the fear. I needed to know why I called in what I did, and this is the deep work I now do in the world.

An important aspect of the law of polarity is that opposites are interdependent—one cannot exist without the other. This is why we have a lot of dependency and codependency in the world. You can't have a dependent person without a codependent person.

For example, you cannot fully appreciate happiness without having experienced sadness. Polarity creates a spectrum of experiences, and it allows people to navigate through a range of emotions and situations that are sometimes extreme.

The more one understands both sides, the more profound their understanding of life becomes and the more ability they have for expansion because their perspective shifts. This law encourages people to shift their perspectives and, when faced with challenges, recognize that the opposite side can provide clarity with solutions.

I could have chosen to stay in the devastation—and trust me, the grief was real—and I did. I felt all the feels. There was no spiritual bypassing there, but I could not fully appreciate the happiness without experiencing the deep sadness. The more we understand both sides, the more profound our understanding of life becomes.

How can you use the law of polarity in your life? By embracing both sides. I completely understand how crazy this sounds, what's going to come next. How difficult it might be to digest, especially if you are actively experiencing trauma. Instead of resisting negative experiences or emotions, acknowledge them, embrace them, and recognize that they are a part of this human experience that allows for deep emotional growth.

By reflecting on challenges when we're confronted with difficulties, we ask ourselves different questions. I say now, instantly, "What do I need to know? What lesson am I learning here?" But I might ask myself what the opposite of the situation might be. For example, if I'm feeling stressed, I consider what peace might feel like or how I can move toward that. Do you have any tools that would even facilitate that?

Then, you want to look at cultivating balance. Strive to find the balance in your life by recognizing when you are leaning too heavily toward one side of the polarity. For instance, if you're giving too much masculine energy, find ways to receive and repent as feminine energy.

Let's break this down. The masculine energy is going to show up in your life with giving. It's the right-hand side of your body; it's the doing, the action. The left-hand side of your body is receiving. It's the feminine, nurturing, creative side. What side are you on? Are you good at executing and delivering? Are you good at receiving and just living in your creative world? You must find ways to receive and replenish both, and this takes mindfulness and awareness.

Practice mindfulness to become aware of your thoughts and emotions around how you have set up the law of polarity in your life and whether it is working for you or against you. This awareness allows you not only to recognize where you're experiencing one side of a polarity but also provides the opportunity to explore its opposite. I find this law to be fascinating because if we know one side, we know the answer to the other. I like to say that it puts us on a playing field to have all the answers available to us. All we need to do is identify.

So, let's talk about reframing the negative experiences. When we're faced with challenges, and maybe we've been faced with challenges our whole lives, we say our life has been nothing but a challenge.

I'm going to challenge you right now to consciously reframe your perspective. Instead of seeing failure as being purely negative, I want you to recognize it as a learning opportunity that contributes to future success. Ask yourself, "What do I need to know? What is it teaching me?" Because nothing is happening repetitively without your contribution and commitment to it.

How might the law of polarity show up in your life? One area is emotional experiences. You might find that periods of sadness or struggle lead to a greater appreciation for happiness and fulfillment. Recognize that these patterns can help you navigate your emotional highs and lows more effectively.

In relationships, you may notice that conflicts or disagreements can often lead to deeper connections and understanding once resolved. Do you allow yourself to resolve conflicts, or do you stay on one side or the other? This contrast helps clarify what you truly value in these relationships. Do you allow yourself to feel vulnerable enough to share and discuss what is important to you? The ego is there to protect, and the law of polarity is no exception. This is an area where there are extremes.

Well, there couldn't be anything more extreme than the ego and heart energy. The ego is there to protect, divide, separate, and judge, and perhaps the heart doesn't recognize this. It just wants to expand. It wants to move forward and connect to love. The ego is about fear-based decisions. The heart is about love-based decisions.

Does it feel like love? Does it feel like fear? Can you see the polarity here, where you might bounce in and out of that? This contrast will help you clarify what you are exhibiting in your life and what you might need to do to shift. With the law of polarity, you want to limit the extreme pendulum swings. It's like closing the gap and straightening the learning curve.

Now let's look at career growth. Experiencing setbacks in your career can highlight your strengths and guide you to new opportunities, and recognizing the duality of success and failure can motivate you to keep pushing forward.

The misconception about the law of polarity is that it's only about good and bad. In reality, it encompasses a wide range of opposites, including joy, sorrow, love, fear, success, and failure.

Some believe that opposites are statistics and unchangeable, and they're unchanging. However, the law of polarity teaches us that everything is fluid, and shifts can occur along the spectrum of experience.

Another misconception is that you must align with one side of the polarity, such as always being positive. In truth, embracing both sides leads to a more balanced and authentic life.

Yet another misconception is that polarity is negative and associated with conflict or struggle. However, acknowledging and understanding polarity can lead to growth, resilience, and a deeper insight into what it is you truly desire.

People often mistakenly think that it's a philosophical idea only, a theatrical concept with no practical application. In fact, it can be a powerful tool for personal development and understanding life's complexities.

Let's face it—life is complicated. We tend to make it even more complicated. When I was 16, I read Scott M. Peck's book, *The Road Less Traveled*. It left a huge impact on me. The first line is: "Life is difficult." I will admit that life was difficult, but it was filled with beautiful moments, too.

In fact, I will take it a step further. Here is a truth I live by: there is an easy way and a hard way, and the universe will support whichever you choose. I lived most of my adult life the hard way, and I didn't realize that was a conscious choice. I now consciously call in the easy way. I am always aware that there are two paths. I have experienced the hard. Now I ask the high vibrational question: "What is the easy way?"

I cultivate a deeper, richer understanding of experiences by keeping it simple and navigating my challenges with grace. This fosters my personal growth because I'm willing to let go of the things that no longer serve me. I recognize the interplay of opposites, which allows for a more balanced, fulfilling life because I choose it.

There are several ways in which opposites contribute to effective problem-solving. We want to enhance perspective, and that's exactly what it does. Recognizing opposites allows individuals to view a problem from different angles.

For example, understanding both the pros and cons of a situation can lead to a more comprehensive analysis and better decision-making. As a Libra, I like to live in a balanced universe. I desire to recognize the yin and yang and the ups and downs because I represent the scale. I'm in a constant balancing act.

Next is identifying extremes. By exploring the extremes of a situation, you can gain clarity on the full range of possibilities. This can help in identifying what is working and what isn't, allowing for a more targeted solution. In other words, by exploring the extremes of what you're feeling, you can identify where you can slow that pendulum down.

Use critical thinking. Consider opposing viewpoints. Such thinking prompts people to question their assumptions and beliefs, which can lead to innovative solutions that may not be considered otherwise. It is an expansion. We're activating the universal law of abundance.

Take a balanced approach to problem-solving. For instance, in a team setting, valuing both assertive and collaborative communication styles can lead to more effective teamwork and better outcomes. It allows for more expansion and compromise.

Understanding that opposite views can coexist helps us find the middle ground. This is particularly useful in negotiations and conflicts, where recognizing the validity of both sides can lead to mutually beneficial solutions. Where in your life are you unmovable and unwavering?

In problem-solving, identifying opposites can clarify what is truly desired versus what is expected. For example, recognizing a feeling of lack can help articulate the need for abundance. If you recognize, "I have a lack in my life," it can guide you toward solutions that fulfill that need.

Embracing the concept allows greater flexibility in thinking. When we do that, we get to move in and out of places that would not be available to us otherwise.

When you understand that situations can change and that multiple outcomes are possible, you are more willing to adapt strategies as new information arises. Do you see where that expansion is available to you right now? In what situations can you use the law of polarity? Where are you stuck in a story? Are you unwavering? Are you angry and unwilling to forgive?

The universal law of polarity can allow you to step out of your story and into someone else's story so you have a deeper understanding of the problem's context. For instance, understanding the difference between short-term and long-term consequences can inform better decision-making and strategic planning.

Never use the words "best," "worst," or "always." Using superlatives like that will not serve you in the life of expansion, abundance, or the law of polarity. It will keep you on one side of the spectrum. Identifying opposites makes you more empowered, informed, and better at making decisions. It provides a clearer view of your potential outcomes and consequences so you can grow exponentially.

You now have both sides to the story, and you can make an educated decision. This plays a critical role in fostering diverse perspectives, encouraging critical thinking, promoting balance, stimulating creativity, and embracing the duality of situations and individuals.

We can all navigate our challenges more effectively with a more well-rounded solution. Who doesn't want that? Do you want to stay stuck? Are you happy being on one side of the law of polarity? This universal law states that everything has an opposite, and everything is available to us. You get to decide how this law is going to work for you.

The opposite of being stuck is movement. The old way of thinking is not going to give you a new way of life. You must implement something new.

I know that may not be a friendly thing to say. I didn't think it was, either, when someone said it to me. In fact, it made me really angry, but guess what? I was stuck on one side because the inner child in me thought that it was safe there.

When I was willing to flip to the other side of understanding that story, my expansion called in the support of what I needed. If we don't call in our support from our story, it will be a never-ending cycle. It will keep us in insecurity, and we will never thrive or create something different if we do not learn that the truth is that we can choose expansion, not limitation.

You can choose good, not bad. You get to choose light, not dark. You get to choose to be powerful, not powerless. You get to choose to embrace, not resist. You can use your unique talents and gifts to work for you, not against you. You get to choose and upgrade your language. You get to speak your life into existence.

Life wants you to manifest. If you're shut down, write a positive version of what it is you want right now. Recognize your challenges and what the opposite of the way you want to feel is. Ask deep, thought-provoking questions: "What beliefs do I hold about abundance or scarcity? How can I shift my perspective to see that opportunities are available to me, especially if I believe that the world is not available to me? What areas of life do I feel limited in? What would the opposite of that life feel like?"

Choose your experiences. You get to choose to expand yourself over your limitations, good over bad, and light over dark. Transcend judgment and step out of your ego. I can't express enough the importance of moving beyond ego-driven judgments and into a space of understanding and acceptance.

We might be holding space for both sides, which we might have needed. We might have needed that ego to protect us for many years, and now we don't. But we're stuck in a never-ending story of it showing up, and we're not willing to look at the other side of the coin because we're afraid.

I can't tell you that the other side may be joy rather than sorrow, success rather than failure, but we don't use judgments. We allow ourselves to hold space for both sides of the coin. The swinging pendulum is a constant ebb and flow, and it will give us a deeper understanding of growth and what we need in our lives.

Here are some practical ways to apply the law of polarity in your life. First, journal about your experiences and identify your opposites. Practice gratitude to recognize abundance. Engage in mindfulness to observe thoughts and feelings without attachment. Write out affirmations that reinforce the understanding of your polarity. I embrace both my strengths and weaknesses. There is no spiritual bypassing. That is not the point of the law of polarity.

The empowered message here is to remind you that everything you desire is already available to you. You simply need to align with what you desire, not what you don't desire. Your call to action here is to understand the insights gained from your personal life, not someone else's. Put a blueprint over your life and embrace the dualities that exist in stepping into your power to create the reality you desire.

If I had not had the life I have experienced, I would not have the understanding, healing, and growth I have now. So, I invite you to question, reflect, and foster an open dialogue and insight into your relationship with the law of polarity.

This law will catapult you forward if you allow it to move openly. That means we do not deny. We stay open to the expansion of understanding: "Ah, I understand that relationship. Oh, I see where that's going. Oh, I feel the reactivity there. That is the pendulum swinging and keeping me over here. And I must look at the other side. Am I willing to embrace that?"

Ask yourself, "Am I willing to embrace a new way of doing things?" The law of polarity teaches us that everything is in a constant state of flux. Joy can turn into sadness. Abundance can shift into scarcity. It deepens our perceptions and choices.

Your right to choose here is where the law of polarity will bounce back and forth for you. If you want it to work for you, you don't have to choose one side. You don't have to reject the negative feelings. In truth, embracing the polarity means accepting both sides of your situation, the good and the bad.

Acceptance is where you allow growth and a more nuanced understanding of your experience. The concept of the law of polarity is sometimes inherently pessimistic, suggesting that it's filled with conflict and struggle. I often get that in my life: "Your life is so full of content, so full of drama, so full of chaos."

In fact, understanding polarity can empower you to find balance and harmony in your life that would not be available otherwise. Recognizing this challenge can lead to exponential growth and transformation. The law of polarity is not just a philosophical idea. It is a concept that allows you to use practical implications and applications. It is a real-world application.

Understanding this law can influence how we approach our thoughts, beliefs, and actions, improve our decision-making, and lead to a deeper connection to ourselves and the universe.

While the law of polarity indicates that opposites exist, it doesn't mean that all opposites are equal in value and effect. That is a misconception. For example, the experience of love may be much more fulfilling than the experience of fear. Recognizing the nuances between opposites can help you make a conscious choice about which energies you want to cultivate.

Another misconception is that polarity is the same as dualism. Dualism presents a binary view of existence, good versus evil. The law of polarity, however, emphasizes the interdependency of opposites and encourages a more holistic understanding of reality in which both sides coexist and inform each other. It isn't one side against the other but open communication.

By clarifying these misconceptions, you can fully appreciate and use this law, and it can lead not only to a more powerful existence but the balance you may have desired all along.

QUESTIONS FOR REFLECTION

Do you allow yourself to resolve conflicts, or do you stay on one side or the other?

_____

_____

_____

Do you allow yourself to feel vulnerable?

_____

_____

_____

Where in your life are you unmovable and unwavering?

_____

_____

_____

Where are you stuck in a story?

_____

_____

_____

What areas of life do you feel limited in?

_____

_____

_____

What would the opposite of that life feel like?

_____

_____

_____

Are you willing to embrace a new way of doing things?

_____

_____

_____

CHAPTER 5

WE DON'T ALWAYS GET WHAT WE WANT, BUT WE GET WHAT WE NEED

THE LAW OF ATTRACTION

"Once you make a decision, the universe conspires to make it happen."
~ Ralph Waldo Emerson

The law of attraction is all about our belief system and the universal principle that like attracts like. This means that the energy and intentions we emit through our thoughts, beliefs, and emotions attract similar energies and experiences in our lives.

So, everything is perfect in the law of attraction. Everything we attract is absolutely what we need. The present is the best time to change our trajectory, but the law of attraction exists whether we believe it or not.

We attract with everything you think, say, and do. Everything is based on our current belief system. Sometimes, we don't know what we need to attract, but someone close to us will attract it for us.

I have had an interesting relationship with the law of attraction my whole life.

It was my daughter's last year in high school, and she desperately wanted a graduation gift. Not just *any* graduation gift. She wanted a male poodle puppy, which she had heard was available. She had chosen to go to Chico State, which was a local college, so I thought perhaps she would live at home with him.

The moment I saw this cute little boy (the poodle), I said yes, and it didn't take more than a day to realize that Leon was **MY** dog. Even though this was her graduation gift, she went off to college, and he stayed with me. It was love at first sight. He was the love of my life. (I want to let you all know that she was good with this as she was off living her best college life.)

Not only did he save my life through the years, but he was my heart, my soul, and my grounding connection. I had no idea what this little boy would mean to me. I believe that the universe delivered him to me to protect, guide, and love me, and he did just that for 16 years.

In case it isn't clear, the universe knew I needed this dog more than I did. This was my first experience of unconditional love. He got me through the biggest heartbreak of my life, and he saved my life on multiple occasions when the migraine medication nearly killed me, barking to wake me up as I teetered over the pool or while standing at the top of a staircase, and grabbing my hair just before I sank into a tub of water and drowned. Yes, Leon saved my life.

Now, where does the law of attraction come in? He was guided to me. There is nothing random about the universe, and there's nothing random in my daughter dragging me to see a dog that I insisted we were not going to get. Our connection was guided, and not a day goes by that I don't feel his presence still.

When it was time for him to go, I held him in my arms as he passed away, and I thanked him and told him how grateful I was for every moment that he was in my life. I sometimes think that he was an angel sent to take care of me. If any of you have ever had a fur baby, then you'll know what I'm talking about.

THE TRUTH WITHIN THE LIE

THE LIE: *What we think we need is not always true.*

THE TRUTH: *We call in everything we need, and everything is divinely guided.*

People think it's enough just to believe the law of attraction, but we have to understand the past and the future and our relationship with them. In essence, we want to look at our most dominant thoughts, the feelings shaping our reality, and the people we attract based on that. The energy and intentions we emit through our beliefs, thoughts, and emotions will attract similar energies and experiences into our lives.

That means that everything we emit, we are going to attract. That is energy, my friends, and energy does not lie. Everything we are and what we show up to, we attract.

We may keep wondering, *"How can I keep attracting that when I'm saying all the right things?"* This is where people trip themselves up with the law of attraction. They might be doing mantras to attract abundance, but their thought process is anchored in a belief system that they haven't addressed yet.

Your most dominant thought will create your life. If you're complaining about your life all the time, you're going to keep attracting negative situations. This is a philosophy that suggests that our positive thoughts and actions lead to positive outcomes, while negative thoughts and actions attract the same.

That is the truth. Our mind creates our reality, and we attract what we think and speak it into existence, whether it's our health, finances, or relationships. Believe it or not, 95% of what we do is subconscious, so we may not be aware of what is sabotaging us.

We activate this law by consciously focusing on what we desire and maintaining a positive mindset. That's how it works: the clarity of intent. We have to clearly define what we want. This is so essential. We have to clearly define what you desire. The more effectively we can align our energy with that, the more we're going to attract it.

Emotional alignment plays a critical role. You must genuinely feel the emotions associated with achieving your desires, such as joy, gratitude, and excitement. Align with it. Pull it in. Act as if it's already happened and celebrate it. Don't fear it and wonder how it's going to play out.

Your belief system must support your desires. If you're holding limiting beliefs about what you can achieve, it will hinder your attraction process. This is essential to cultivating a mindset that embraces abundance and possibility.

Most people get tripped up here. They're on the playing field, saying, "I'm activating it," but their belief system is not aligned at all. This is where the universal law of polarity comes into play, where we accept, challenge, incorporate, and understand why that polarity exists.

If we want to use the law of attraction in our daily lives, we must start setting intentions. We want to have clear intentions every day as to what we wish to attract. This can be related to your career, relationships, health, personal growth, or whatever it is you desire. Desire is the key component here.

I'm going to take a moment here to reinforce the importance of practicing gratitude. It is in every universal law. Regularly expressing gratitude for what you already have raises your vibrational frequency and aligns you with positive energy, making it easier to attract more good things into your life.

It's also important to visualize your desires and goals as if they've already been achieved. Create a vivid mental picture and immerse yourself in the associated emotions. This is what I do. Anytime I go on stage, I create a vivid mental picture that removes all fear and puts me in a transcendental state that is associated with the emotions that I want to emit.

Positive affirmations reinforce your beliefs and your intentions. Repeat statements that align with your desires. This helps you to reprogram your subconscious mind. If you keep saying, "I'm not going to have it," "I can't afford it," or "It'll never happen," then you won't attract it.

You must be aligned with your affirmations, and you must choose and repeat that alignment with your subconscious mind. That means you have to challenge your subconscious. You have to be aware of what it's saying and how it's showing up. You do that by looking at your day-to-day life. Are your actions aligning with what you're claiming?

If we want to attract love but haven't done it yet, how are we showing up every day? Are we showing up with our ego energy protecting us so no one can actually ever find us? It is really important in the universal law of attraction to look at how our life is playing out. What are we attracting? What is it we desire to attract? This mindfulness allows us to stay aware of our thoughts and emotions throughout the day.

I love to set a timer on my phone. It interrupts my thoughts, allowing me to assess what I'm thinking. Is it supporting the life I desire? If your thoughts do not support the life you desire, you will not activate the universal law of attraction.

Now, to activate the law of attraction, we can do several things.

One is to make a vision board. I call them "clarity boards," and they're great for making a visual representation of your goals and desires using images, words, and symbols. Place it where you can see it daily and remind yourself of your intentions. However, if you do this with a belief system that's never going to happen, you're back to square one.

Gratitude journals are another tool. Write down everything that you're grateful for each day, a practice that shifts your focus from lack to abundance.

However, if you still believe that achieving what you want is not possible and you think, *"If I just keep doing this, I'm going to override my negative relationship with lack and fear,"* it's not going to work. You have to acknowledge where you are.

The law of polarity goes hand in hand with the law of vibration. Meditating to clear your mind and visualize your desires is very powerful. I love this practice because it raises your vibrational frequency and aligns you with your goals. It takes you into a conscious state of being.

"Emotional Freedom Technique, or EFT," is also effective. It involves tapping your meridian points, focusing your attention on your desires and releasing limited beliefs. Louise Hay introduced this technique to me years ago, and it can help clear emotional blocks that hinder attraction.

Another technique is positive reinforcement. Surround yourself with positive influences, such as uplifting books and podcasts and supportive people who encourage your growth and aspirations. Challenging yourself to grow and expand plants new spiritual seeds in your life.

Next, let's look at what hinders the activation of the law of attraction.

First are negative thought patterns. Constantly focusing on negative outcomes, doubts, and fears keeps you in the grind and will only attract more negativity into your life. This often results in a deeply seated negative belief. Is it possible to shift that? One zillion percent, yes.

Another thing that can keep you from activating the law of attraction is inconsistent focus. Fluctuating between positive and negative thoughts can disrupt the attraction process. Consistency is key to manifesting your desires. This means acknowledging and incorporating all of your story, not bits and pieces. Ignoring parts of your story will never lead to an abundant life.

The next obstacle is resistance to change. This is a big one. Holding on to old patterns, beliefs, or comfort zones can block the flow of any new opportunity. Resistance can stem from fear of the unknown or change. This is what I call the "terror barrier."

Everything on one side is new and expansive, but your ego comes in and says, "We don't know that, so we're not going to choose that." So, this resistance to change may, in fact, be resistance to something new.

We tend not to trust the new, and we attract what we know. Even if it does not give us the outcome we want, it is familiar. That is what I call the "home zone." That is our comfort zone. Nothing will grow there.

Your home zone is where everything expands, and you must choose to believe that everything is available to you and focus on clear purposes and goals that will improve your life. You must choose it.

We often don't ponder what we attract, and we build stories that go out into the world. That is our narrative. My worthiness message used to be, "I'll never rise up." If we believe that we will never rise, then that is what will happen, no matter what we desire.

Many of us will receive a different message than what is true. The lie is: "I could have done that, but my worthiness level came in and sabotaged me. My belief system didn't support my true potential."

I want you to be grateful for where you are. I want you to shift from "what I have to" to "what I get to."

I want you to visualize where you want to be every day. I want you to see and believe that to be true for yourself. I want you to tap into stories that sabotage you.

Perhaps it's: "I'll never be a millionaire. I don't even know how to do it."

So, you'll sabotage yourself. "There have never been millionaires in my family." Maybe this is what the story is about. "I wouldn't know what to do with that kind of money." Maybe the story goes on to even say that. Ground yourself and get clear on what you want.

You don't need to know the way to practice and activate this law. What you do need to do is ground yourself and get very clear on what you want.

You need to activate what you desire. What are you willing to trust and believe will happen in your life? You need to know it's all available to you. Take action and ditch what's holding you back. Let it go.

Use the universal law of sacrifice and implement the new law of vibration, but also look at what reinforces this law. What reinforces the law of attraction? You do. You are the key component here.

You are the law of attraction. It is everything you believe, speak, say, and feel. You activate it all. Your belief system is how you're going to show up in the world and how you are going to see, want, and claim it all.

So, I want you to acknowledge and celebrate your progress right now. Even if you don't have the results yet, if you are open to this knowledge, celebrate the steps you're willing to take today.

Believing and taking action every day is key. Every day, wake up and wash, rinse, repeat. This is never a one-and-done, my friends. This is using mantras: "I am worthy of receiving. I am worthy of attracting."

Why is this so important to you? This law empowers you to take control of your thoughts and energy, leading to intentionally manifesting positive changes in all areas of your life. Why would you not want to activate this? You attract in your life what aligns with your belief system and your mindset.

Choosing is your greatest power, allowing you to shift to success and abundance by activating every universal law. Think of it as a high-energy vibration that comes out of nowhere and that you actually activate.

The tool here is simple: you get to decide.

You get to decide whether you want to reinforce your life positively by asking yourself, "What might hinder the activation of my law of attraction?" You get to acknowledge your negative thought patterns. You get to choose clarity and identify one thing that you can do today.

You get to stay inconsistent with your focus, making excuses, or you get to say, "This is what I am capable of doing," and claim it today. Don't fluctuate between what was and what is. Claim what lets you use the past as rocket fuel for your life today. What can that build in your life?

Many people feel frustrated when they don't see immediate results. Then, they start self-doubting, which can create more inner conflict. The vast amount of information on the law of attraction can be overwhelming, leading to some confusion about how it can be applied effectively.

I'm going to say it again: to handle these frustrations, practice patience.

If you're impatient and think, "*I need it now,*" understand that manifestation requires time and constant effort. Trust the timing of your journey. Trust your process.

Trust is a huge part of this law. I want you to seek support. Consider joining a community or finding a mentor who understands the law of attraction. Sharing experiences can provide encouragement, motivation, and understanding of where you are, what movement you need to make, and perhaps where you're stuck. I believe that people are never stuck, but your belief systems are.

This is why it's important to identify and challenge your limiting beliefs in your journal. Keep it simple. Do not get overwhelmed with the old stories. Tap into them and determine how you can move forward. No one is stuck. No one is ever stuck. Thoughts may be stuck in a repetitive cycle because they've kept you safe, but once you understand and activate this law, your growth will be exponential.

And stay committed. Consistency is key here. Commit to a daily practice that aligns with your desires, even when it feels challenging. You don't abandon ship. You focus on your small wins and celebrate your successes along the way. That builds your confidence and reinforces the effectiveness of the law of attraction.

Understanding this law can shift your mindset so that it aligns with your desires, creating a life of exponential personal growth. Recognize and address the hindrances in your life, and then realize that by using this law, you can create a life of abundance and expansion. Your truth will be that your past only feeds into what you desire now. It only supports you. There are no limitations in your life.

You may want to write out a brief story about how the law of attraction has played a role in your life and how you thought about something, and it came to fruition. Also, explore why your daily thought process has not given you what you desire. Write out, "This is what I do daily. This is what I believe to be true."

Everything can be flipped. Everything can be rewired. Everything is cosmic lasagna. Layered and messy.

The universal truth is that to give is to receive. So, what are you willing to give back to the universe using the universal law of sacrifice?

Again, you are no exception to this rule. Everything is available to you. How can you activate the law of attraction in your life?

QUESTIONS FOR REFLECTION

What are you attracting?

_____

_____

_____

What is it you desire to attract?

_____

_____

_____

What might hinder the activation of the law of attraction in your life?

_____

_____

_____

What are you willing to give back to the universe using the universal law of sacrifice?

_____

_____

_____

How can you activate the law of attraction in your life?

_____

_____

_____

CHAPTER 6
UNIVERSAL LAW OF ALIGNMENT
THE AWAKENING

"Fail early, fail often, but always fail forward."
~ John C. Maxwell.

Your life depends on understanding that everything is working for you, not against you. From my perspective and from years of suffering, I now understand that my body not only kept the score, but I had to unlock the emotional trauma that it stored in order to understand why it was rebelling. There was no way around this.

I was diagnosed with intractable migraines. In fact, the doctors at UCFS said I was in the top 2%. There wasn't much they could do for me back in the '80s. There weren't many treatment options available then—no triptans, ergots, CGRP inhibitors, or even Botox, which is now approved for chronic migraines. What they resorted to were beta blockers, antidepressants, and anticonvulsants. The CGRP inhibitors were not introduced until 2018. You name it, they gave it to me. If I didn't take the medication, I would be considered uncooperative and discharged.

I sought out every holistic answer—having never taken an aspirin in my life—traveling far and wide across the world in pursuit of cutting-edge research. Eventually, I found myself in Victoria, Canada, attending a two-week alternative medicine retreat. It was deep work, intimate, and life-changing. It took me years to recognize and use the modalities that I was taught. Through acupuncture, Hellerwork, and other functional modalities, my body released an explosion of unexpected trauma that I didn't know was still being stored.

I didn't experience a migraine for the next six weeks after I returned home. Previously, I had been hospitalized for up to 10 days at a time every month—put into comas, given doses of medication that could have killed an elephant—and I never went 72 hours without pain.

Back to the retreat in Victoria. I flew off a yoga mat during my first meditation and said, "I don't think I'm a Republican." This was a huge revelation. Let me remind you that I worked for a pro-business lobbyist group for years. At the time, I had no idea how important what I said meant—I was waking up. I had been in a deep sleep, never asking what I wanted or what I truly believed in. I realized I was never asking the questions that would open the doors to my healing. The ones that truly mattered to me. That was the beginning.

I recognized that I had never asked myself, "What do I want to be in this life?" I was working and navigating out of a place of external validation. If the world were happy with me, I was going to do incredible things with that. So, I was constantly out of alignment with my truth.

My first reflective question to you is: Are you in alignment with your truth?

I grew up in an extremely conservative household. Being raised like that, I did not know that I could make my own choices. I never considered that I wouldn't be a Republican. I did exactly what any good soldier would do: go out into the world and share the mission and voice that I had been taught. This limited any exploration of my desires and aspirations. Let me add that this has nothing to do with politics and everything to do with allowing and giving ourselves permission to navigate from a place of truth. My truth was shut down, gaslit, and questioned at every turn.

THE LIE: *I would find my value in how people received and embraced me. Any form of conflict I would try to fix, and abandon myself.*

THE TRUTH: *My body was rebelling and trying to understand the polarity of these two worlds and how they could co-exist. I eventually realized that I was not wrong for having a different opinion.*

This illustrates the deep connection between physical health and inner alignment. Inspirational teacher Louise Hay explains this relationship in her book, *Heal Your Body*.

I invite you to consider this thought-provoking question: Are you in alignment with your truth? Examine where you are in your life right now. Is it where you thought you would be? Did you compromise? Did you sacrifice? Did you stay the course? Did you ever even consider what it was you desired in the first place?

The law of aligned action states that taking actions that resonate with your true, authentic self leads to a sense of fulfillment and purpose. If you aren't clear on who you are, everything you connect to is going to be off, too.

If you're off by just a single degree, you can end up miles off course. For example, if your plane's course is off by one degree, you're going to hit a different island. So, if you're out of alignment by one degree with your truth, you aren't ever going to connect with any aligned action. This is why this law is so important to activate and align with.

Now, let's discuss the spiritual practice of this law. I can't stress enough that engaging in aligned action is not just a practical endeavor; it is a spiritual practice that connects profoundly with our core beliefs and deepest desires. We cannot achieve our desired results by connecting with someone else's beliefs. If we do, we will always make mistakes.

One of the universal laws that supports aligned action is the law of attraction. Aligning your actions with your intentions enhances the manifestation process, drawing supportive energies that resonate with your desires.

The second one is the law of correspondence: when you evolve internally, your external circumstances transform in kind. Engaging in aligned action elevates your vibrational frequency, which, in turn, attracts positive experiences in harmony with your true essence. The law of cause and effect illustrates how every action taken in alignment generates corresponding outcomes, reinforcing the significance of intentionality in the choices you make.

This is why it's important to allow circumstances to unfold naturally. When your actions are aligned with your true desires, you create a flow of energy that facilitates manifestation. You cannot manifest without using these laws in harmony and alignment.

There are **Five Steps of Aligned Action**.

1. **Identify the Truth.** When I woke up in that holistic clinic, I was dealing with migraines that destroyed my quality of life. My truth wasn't anything that I understood. No one ever asked me my truth, and I was out of alignment. So number one, you need to identify your truth. Deeply reflect on your beliefs, desires, and values. What is it you truly want to achieve? Are they even your desires, values, dreams, and beliefs, or have you taken on someone else's? What does it mean for you to be in alignment with your truth at this stage in your life?
2. You need to **Set Clear Goals** that resonate authentically with your truth. They must not be rigid, but adaptable and flexible.

3. **Acknowledge Your Challenges**. Identify potential obstacles that you may encounter in this journey toward enlightenment—because when you align, enlightenment occurs. Recognize that these challenges are essential for formulating effective strategies to overcome them. Ask yourself, "What obstacles have I faced in my pursuit of my true desires?"
4. **Flip the Narrative**. We're going to use a little bit of the universal law of polarity here. I want you to reframe negative thoughts or setbacks as opportunities for personal growth. Look at the mindset shift that you're focusing on, learning from, and experiencing not as a failure but as a successful process. I want insights and anecdotes on how you are flipping this narrative and how it has positively impacted your life.
5. Make **Regular Check-ins** on your progress and periodically adjust your mindset. Self-reflection and evaluations of your alignment are essential. Ask yourself, "Do I take the time to check in with myself to ensure that I am remaining aligned with my truth?" Every morning, I look in the mirror and say, "Dana, what do you need for me today?" Then I ask, "Is that true? Do I need that?" The answer comes from my intuition, and it's usually a "hell, yes" or a "hell, no."

Living in alignment with your genuine desires and beliefs not only fosters a more fulfilling and healthier existence but also encourages personal empowerment. This empowering nature of aligned action enables you to take control of your life by making conscious choices. And what should it resonate with? Your authenticity. That is going to activate universal desire, which is going to connect you with the idea that everyone yearns for a meaningful and fulfilling life.

These five steps—identify the truth, set clear goals, acknowledge the challenges, flip the narrative, and make regular check-ins—weave together like a tapestry to support one another.

You want to take a hard look at how your life has been built up to this point. Reflect on the **Four Pillars** of **Body, Mind, Spirit,** and **Environment.**

How do these four pillars interact and influence your life? If you're looking at the law of alignment, these four pillars are going to give you structure. Think of it as a blueprint that you're following with balance and harmony.

Each of these pillars is independent of the other. So first, I want you to reflect on them. How are they set up in your life? Do you even have them set up in your life?

Second, I want you to set daily, clear intentions that align with your overarching goals and desires. Does your belief system say they are doable, or have you created something that isn't doable because you don't have the four pillars in place?

The gratitude practice is number three. Gratitude fosters a positive mindset and attracts the supportive energies you need to align.

Number four is mindfulness and presence. Practicing mindfulness will help you remain grounded in the present moment, and this is where all your true power lies. Stay with your truth, as it is from your truth that you get your authentic voice. Your greatest power comes from that—the right to choose—and then you can take aligned action.

Next, let's talk about your support systems. Who is supporting you? Are you alone? Who are your five people? They say that the five people who surround you, you acclimate to. I believe that to be true. I have five seats at my kitchen table of people I talk to—like Maya Angelou and my father—and this is my support system. These are people, living or dead, whom you can lean on and with whom your higher self can have discussions.

I guarantee you that by surrounding yourself with supportive energies that uplift and encourage you, you will not only align with your personal growth, but you will also start calling in people who align with you and your external world.

But it starts with your internal voice, your internal belief system of who it is you want and who it is you're listening to. Claiming your truth means progressing with intention and confidence. Your call to action here is to take immediate steps towards alignment.

I want to remind you that this journey is ongoing and not merely a destination. Don't wait to get there. Aligned action puts you on the playing field. Every micro step you take moves you closer.

Every time you can claim your life and speak into existence what you desire, your emotional, intellectual, and spiritual expansion is exponential. I want you to evoke a strong emotional connection by sharing a heartfelt story that has moved you up to this point in your life. Stay in your truth.

Listen to what you call in. Listen to your interactions with the people you have already called into your external world. Does this truth force conformity? Are you able to think, speak, feel, and act toward your truth? Is it embraced? Is it supported? Are you in alignment with your truth, where you won't get lost in uncertainty and second-guess yourself? Or do you place your truth in external validation and give all your power away?

I'm here to tell you that no one has a more intimate relationship with you than *you*. This law, aligned action, is about moving forward with trust and purpose. It can shift and change your life immediately. No waiting, no delay. It's here and now.

You also need to clean up your vibrational matches. Look at the world around you. Look at the people you've called in. Where can you clean up your vibrational matches? Energy is everything, and energetically, you are calling in every structure that you need to flourish.

Ask yourself, "What do I need to sacrifice to create the life I want and align with what my truth is? What do I need to give up? Where am I resisting change? Where do I need to pivot that one degree? What do I think about that? Is that enough?"

I want you to look at where you have evoked a strong emotion around your truth and what that looks like when we put it back to the four pillars. The truth is that living in alignment means living in harmony with your true desires and beliefs and leading a healthier, more fulfilled life. Isn't that what you're here to do, to be more connected to your truth?

Understand that aligned action is going to help you be more conscious and purposeful in your decision-making. It's going to lead to an overall well-being that will activate the law of attraction, calling in what you truly desire.

So, again, are the four pillars—body, mind, spirit, and environment—in alignment? Set goals and understand the process of how this matters. Confront challenges and flip the narrative when needed. And do regular check-ins with yourself to ensure you're in alignment.

When it comes to this law, we often look at the circumstances that have happened in our lives already. That might explain why this law doesn't work for you. See if you can identify with this. Maybe you feel frustrated that you're not manifesting. You feel constantly overwhelmed, irritated, and dissatisfied with your life choices or circumstances. The task that once brought joy may now feel burdensome. This persistent feeling of frustration could be due to the fact that you're not manifesting correctly because you're not aligned with your truth.

Another sign that you're not using the law of aligned action is realigned action. I want you to reflect on the source of your frustration. Identify specific areas where your actions are misaligned with your true desires. Consider journaling about what genuinely excites you, not what excites someone else. What excites you? Are you listening to your truth?

The second reason people don't use this law is that they lack clarity or direction. You may find yourself drifting aimlessly. Maybe you're feeling uncertain about what you truly want in life. I often describe this feeling as being lost in the desert. You're in perfection paralysis. You can't decide because you're afraid of being wrong.

To realign this action, take time to engage in self-reflection. Create a clarity board—often called a vision board—to visually represent your goals and aspirations. This can help you clarify your intentions and provide a tangible reminder of what it is you are aligned with. You might be surprised if you are drawn energetically to something as you're making a vision board. I often encourage my clients to pick it, whether they know what it means or not, if they're drawn to it and do not second-guess it, but put it on their board.

A year before I co-founded Califlour Foods, a ready-made cauliflower pizza crust company, I put on my vision board the image of a huge white cauliflower. Now, cauliflower isn't my favorite vegetable, so I wasn't sure why I put it on my board.

I didn't second-guess because I was telling my clients not to do that, either. I cut my huge cauliflower out, and I put it right in the middle of my board. I couldn't believe what that led to a year later. People like to poo-poo these clarity boards, but I can't tell you how powerful it is when your intention is behind it, you don't second-guess, and you align your actions with what you want. So, get out of your monkey brain, pick out what you desire, and put it on that board.

On that board, I traveled everywhere, cooking in six countries. I had no desire or vision to do any of that. I ended up hosting retreats and cooking in Italy and going to Amsterdam, Iceland, and France.

Next, we want to examine the physical symptoms of stress. Chronic stress may manifest as headaches, fatigue, and other physical ailments, indicating that your body is reacting to misalignment in your life.

For decades, I lived with intractable migraines, as I was not aligned with my truth or purpose at all. When I realigned my actions, the migraine stopped, and I could incorporate mindful practices such as meditation, yoga, and deep breathing exercises into my routine.

These practices can help you connect with your body, reducing stress and realigning you with energies that are, once again, your true self. It's about getting in alignment. Your body has energy sections—chakras—and it is important to identify where you are feeling things in your body so you can reconnect.

The next sign that you are not using the law of aligned action is procrastination. You might notice a tendency to procrastinate on important tasks. This is due to not being focused on or connected to what you truly desire.

To realign this action, break down your goals into smaller, more manageable steps. Establish a daily routine that includes dedicated time for taking action, no matter how small, celebrating each step you take. This celebration reinforces the habit of moving forward.

Another thing that will hold you back is being overwhelmed by external expectations. You may experience a sense of obligation to meet others' expectations, whether it's family, brands, or society. To counter this, engage in self-affirmation techniques to reinforce the right to pursue your truth regardless of external pressures. You must give yourself permission to set boundaries and put yourself first.

The next indicator that you are not using the law of aligned action is negative thought patterns. You might find yourself caught in a cycle of negative self-talk and limited beliefs, doubting your abilities and feeling undeserving of everything you desire. To realign your actions, use positive affirmations to counteract negative thoughts.

Again, this is not a one-and-done, but you must upgrade your speech. Speak your life into existence, just as you have done with the negative self-talk. We're going to flip that with the law of polarity, using positive, empowering self-talk. Create a list of empowering statements that reinforce your worth and capabilities. I guarantee you that you're more capable and worthy than you can imagine. Repeat these every day to shift your mindset.

The next indicator is difficulty in relationships, conflicts, and misunderstandings with loved ones. To realign, communicate openly with those around you about feelings and desires. This means your ego cannot run the show and protect you. You have to be authentic and willing to be vulnerable, and you must engage in active listening to understand others' perspectives while remaining true to yourself.

Seek relationships that support and uplift your journey to alignment.

Remember, however, there is no destination. The only expectation is that you show up and support yourself.

This is why regular self-reflection is so important. Set time aside each week for it. Ask yourself about your current actions. Check in with yourself about alignment and ask, "Am I doing what I truly desire?" Journal about the powerful tools you can use in this process. Go back and reread your journal and notes.

Be mindful about incorporating daily practices to cultivate present-moment awareness. Seek out communities that resonate with your values. These are all choices you make. You're still making them subconsciously.

Use your visualization techniques to imagine yourself living in alignment with your desires. Picture the actions that you would take and the feelings associated with your achieved goals. Step into that space.

Create this mental image. It might motivate you to take tangible steps in that direction because you are activating a feeling. You can experience what that will feel like. This is a very powerful step in aligning with yourself and your desires.

I want you to consider finding an accountability partner or coach who can support you on this journey toward alignment. Regular check-ins can help you stay focused and motivated and realign you when you start to drift.

Maintaining gratitude on a daily basis is another important practice. Not only does it shift your mindset, but it helps you recognize the positive elements that are already aligned with your true self and available to you.

By recognizing the signs of misalignment, we can get back in realignment and call in the other universal laws to support this journey with greater clarity, purpose, and fulfillment. Re-engaging with the law of alignment empowers people to take the steps that resonate with their true selves, leading to more harmonious, enriched lives.

That is the basis of the law of alignment: embracing and loving your true self and accepting the truth of your desires, not resisting. It's leaning in, not out, and cleaning up any vibrational matches around you that don't align with what you desire.

Don't lose sight of the mission, which includes daily growth and reflection. Be grateful for growth and support it. Align with your truth, actions, and energy.

Once you know your challenges, use the law of attraction to flip your script. Use the law of polarity. Be an overcomer. Define and set clear goals. These goals are not do-or-die. It's about the process of getting there.

I want you to identify the challenges in your way. Use the four pillars of body, mind, spirit, and environment. Where can you find them in your life? Perhaps write out one word expressing what they look like in your life now.

And don't neglect spirituality. We want to make sure that we connect with something greater than ourselves. The seeds of spirituality will support us in your our pillars of alignment. This is the aligned action that can shift and change our lives, moving them forward with exponential growth.

QUESTIONS FOR REFLECTION

What is it you truly want to achieve?

_____

_____

_____

What does it mean for you to be in alignment with your truth at this stage in your life?

_____

_____

_____

What obstacles have you faced in my pursuit of your true desires?"

_____

_____

_____

How are the four pillars—body, mind, spirit, and environment—set up in your life?

_____

_____

_____

Are you listening to your truth?

_____

_____

_____

Are you doing what you truly desire?

_____

_____

_____

CHAPTER 7
LAW OF CAUSE AND EFFECT
THE HEADACHES, THE MEDICATION, THE LEGS

"Nothing comes from nothing."
~ Parmenides

I almost lost my life...

The medication that I thought was saving me was killing me. I was taking 20,000 mg of injectable Demerol a month, and that's not including the anti-vomiting medicines that stabilized me. This ended up causing me to eventually develop 17 forms of staph infections in my legs. The number one question I often get is if I got MRSA. Nope. It was probably the only one I didn't get, but I did get one that didn't need air to grow, and it was rapidly eating away my tissue and muscle.

The terror in my body was visceral. I thought I was going to lose my legs and my life. At that moment, I had a conversation with God that if I kept my legs, I would devote my life to healing. I want to add that I had no idea what that would look like: emotional, physical, or how to navigate it because I was still sick.

So, the healing began. Standing in my kitchen, I tore up a refill prescription. I knew that I was going to die if I took any more medication. When I was in the hospital, I used to have to sign a form saying that I was aware that I could die. That the level of medication could take me. It's hard to believe today what I lived through, what I survived. I endured more pain than any human should ever have to experience.

But one thing was clear: I had to make a different choice. I had to find another way—and I did.

I felt immense gratitude for keeping my legs—all my focus was on that. I began a new chain of cause and effect by changing my practices and mindset. I had no idea what I was going to do. I had no outcome. I had no solution. I just chose not to identify with an old narrative, and my body and mind shifted.

Now, as crazy as it sounds, my life changed, and I created a new chain of healthy cause and effect. I took a leap of faith, and I initiated a new path. What I want you to understand about cause and effect is that you don't need a story as in-depth as mine to activate it. It's a simple law.

THE LIE: *Medication was saving my life, and if I didn't take it, I would die.*

THE TRUTH: *Medication was masking my life and killing me. I live with my legs every day as a reminder of the cause and effect. I want to add that I am forever grateful that I was able to keep my legs.*

For every action, there is a reaction. Life is constructed from a sequence of consequences, a series of interconnected events that shape our reality. I had no idea that medicine would shape my reality. I had no idea that medicine would change my legs. I had no idea that putting that medicine down would change my life and its trajectory.

We often resist outcomes, hoping to control the unpredictable nature of life, but embracing this law means accepting that we will receive what we put out into the universe. If we're resisting something, we're putting that out there. If we're seeking something, we're putting that out there. If we're desiring something, we're putting that out there. If we are negotiating with something, we're putting that out there.

I want you to look at the law of cause and effect and how it presents a different narrative in different areas of your life. It offers freedom, a release from the dark cloud that hovers over you, reminding you that everything you experience is a direct result of specific causes. Everything and every event is a continuation of previous causes and conditions. Nothing is random. Believe it or not, you have called it all in.

This universal law is crucial because every decision we've made up until this point has led to our current reality. To change our circumstances, we must examine the causes behind them. By taking accountability for our choices, we can break negative patterns and initiate a pathway toward better results.

It is essential to remember that changing causation may not immediately affect those around us, but it will fundamentally alter our paths. Now, I couldn't change the relationships that were damaged through my years of illness and medication, such as with my three daughters. I cannot change that impact. I cannot change how that altered their lives. Changing the medication changed my life, which impacted their lives, but I cannot go back and fix it because causation was already in effect.

This process can be likened to a cosmic reset. I often refer to it as "cosmic lasagna," where layers of chaos and order intersect, creating a complex but beautiful structure of life if we allow it. For example, I believed the lie that I needed the medication to manage my pain, which ultimately led to severe consequences.

The painful truth was that the medication was detrimental to my health. It was killing me. I was going to die, and I was hurting the relationships in my life because I could not let go of it. I thought it was saving me. That was a lie. The truth was that it was killing me.

To initiate a new cause-and-effect dynamic, it's vital to remain open to change and stay out of victim mode. Taking responsibility for our circumstances empowers us to rebuild trust not only with ourselves but with others. It takes time.

Consequences accompany each action we take, and understanding this helps us navigate our lives with greater intention and releases us from the shame of our decisions and actions that we've taken. Rebuilding trust starts with accountability, and that starts with us.

Life can feel overwhelming, as though we're thrown into it without any tools at our disposal. Yet, it is our responsibility to learn about the universal laws and recognize that when we know better, we do better. That is a universal law: when we know better, we are required to do better. However, we have to give ourselves love and compassion for what we did not know.

Positive actions expand our lives, while the power to choose always resides within us. This is where people get stuck. They could have chosen differently. Well, could they have? Did they have anything else they could have chosen? This is where grace comes in. Embracing accountability and forgiveness cultivates love and compassion for ourselves, steering us away from defensive behaviors that can lead to offensive and defensive cycles.

Offense and defense will never move you forward. If you want a different result, you must take a different action. And I'm going to say it again: rebuilding trust starts with accountability. Embracing accountability and forgiveness not only cultivates love and compassion for yourself, but it allows you to pay it forward in an unimaginable way. It starts with visualizing what it would feel like to have love and compassion for the version of you who made those decisions.

As I reflect on my journey, I want to invite you to consider your own life. What chains of cause and effect are you experiencing? Are there areas where you feel stuck, perhaps due to past decisions or external influences?

Acknowledge the power you hold within to create a new narrative. Embrace the understanding that every action you take right now can lead to a more fulfilling and empowered existence. Aligning your choices with your true desires and values is your greatest power. With it, you can initiate a transformational journey that reflects the essence of the law of cause and effect.

This is a beautiful law that underlines much of our understanding of the universe, but several common misconceptions about it can hinder a true understanding of its implications. One of these is that it only applies to negative outcomes.

Well, I took the medicine, and I almost died. My legs were badly scarred, so badly that they scare people at first. I have had to work through shame for years on the daily. That was pretty negative karmic action, but the reality is that the law applies to both positive and negative actions.

Every decision and action, whether beneficial or harmful, creates a ripple effect that influences future outcomes. Positive actions can lead to positive results, just as negative actions can lead to adverse consequences.

Another misconception is that every cause will produce an immediate and visible effect. Well, the reality is that the effect may not be immediate or obvious. Sometimes, the consequences of our actions unfold over time, and it can take a while to see the results of our choices. Patience is often required to witness the impact of our actions. We see this with addiction and recovery. What we want for people and what they want for themselves are not aligned.

The next misconception is that the relationship between cause and effect is a simple one. Many people assume that the law operates in a straightforward, linear manner. Nope. The reality is that the relationship is often complex and influenced by multiple factors. Many variables can contribute to an outcome, meaning that the same cause may lead to a different effect under varying circumstances. Allow for variance to take place in your life.

The fourth misconception is that everything happens for a reason. Some interpret the law of cause and effect as suggesting that every event or situation is preordained or has a specific reason behind it.

No. The reality is that while actions lead to consequences, not every event is purposeful or intended. Life can involve randomness and unpredictability, and not all experiences have an inherent meaning.

The next misconception is that inaction has no consequences. Some people believe that failing to act or being passive will not lead to any consequences. Well, the reality is that inaction is also a choice and can lead to its own set of consequences. For instance, failing to address a problem can result in the situation worsening over time. The decision not to act is an action with potential effects that can sometimes even be larger than taking action.

The next misconception is that the law of cause and effect is punitive. Well, there's a perception that this law is about punishment for wrongdoing, making it seem harsh and unforgiving. The reality is that this law is neutral. It simply describes the natural order of cause and effect without moral judgment. It allows one to understand the connections between actions and their consequences rather than enforcing punishment.

This next misconception is a big one: the law of cause and effect is identical to karma. While karma has its basis in cause and effect, it is often interpreted as a moral framework that implies moral retribution. The law of cause and effect is broader, encompassing all actions and their consequences, regardless of moral implications.

The next misconception is that the law eliminates free will, suggesting that we are merely products of our past actions. The reality is that while our past actions influence our present circumstances, we still possess the ability to make choices and take new actions.

Understanding the law empowers us to make conscious choices that can change our future. The next misconception is that the law of cause and effect only pertains to individual actions and responsibilities. The reality is that it also encompasses collective actions and societal influences. Group dynamics, cultural context, and environmental factors all play a role in creating outcomes and highlighting the interconnectedness of cause and effect on multiple levels. We are never alone. We are all internally connected.

What I'd like you to do is examine the causes behind your situation right now. You can change the causation and achieve bigger and better results by being aligned with your truth. Taking accountability and owning your truth helps break negative causation. Also, know that changing this causation may not affect others, but it will change your path. This will represent a cosmic reset.

When I talk about cosmic lasagna, think about all that energy flying around out there, but you get to stay in your power, taking responsibility for your circumstances—no one else's, only yours—rebuilding the trust, and creating a new chain of cause and effect.

Life is not linear, but you can choose and redesign it anytime you want. Doesn't today feel like a good day to look at your relationship to cause and effect and how it's had an effect on your life, recognizing that your reality reflects your beliefs and that the cause you initiate leads to the results you receive—and that putting out abundant results only allows you to receive abundant results?

There is no inherent good or bad in the universe. The universe is neutral. Good and bad are only perceptions of your actions. Ego energy is what comes in to divide, separate, judge, and protect. The heart just wants to expand. It asks you, "What does love feel like? And what would be the cause and effect of adapting that new concept today?" So, remember that the ego divides, separates, and judges. It is there to protect. It will not activate cause and effect effectively, but it will keep you protected and in a loop of the same patterns.

What I'd like you to do is focus on your daily actions for one week. Write down your actions each day to understand what you're creating. This is how powerful you are. Everything up to this point in your life, you've created. Reflect on the principle that what you sow, you shall reap. Find scripture to support this law. Think about actionable steps that align with your desired success. Everything out there aligns with what you are doing. You will get a desired or undesired reaction.

Significant changes involve taking ownership of all aspects of your life: the good, the bad, and the shameful. There's no spiritual bypassing here. Step into faith and trust this process because you do not know the outcome of a new action that you're taking. It's going to be nerve-wracking because you are stepping over the terror barrier, but I want you to feel and believe that you have the power to change your results.

Right now, I want you to write down three empowering statements that will activate your causation and lead to the effect you desire.

QUESTIONS FOR REFLECTION

What chains of cause and effect are you experiencing?

_____

_____

_____

Are there areas where you feel stuck, perhaps due to past decisions or external influences?

_____

_____

_____

CHAPTER 8

DO YOU BELIEVE YOU'RE WORTH IT?

THE LAW OF COMPENSATION

"The universe operates through dynamic exchange... Giving and receiving are different aspects of the flow of energy in the universe."
~ Deepak Chopra

The law of compensation is a powerful universal principle that giving and receiving are in balance. It teaches us that the value we provide to others directly correlates with what we receive in return.

The most intimate relationship you're ever going to have is with yourself. I want you to read that again. Getting to know yourself on a soul level and identifying the ego has everything to do with the law of compensation. Because 95% of what you're telling yourself comes from the subconscious, and 85% of that is negative, you might try to be positive, but your energy won't match. How many times have you met someone, but what they're saying doesn't match what you're feeling, and you can't quite put your finger on it? It's all about the energy.

When I co-founded my first company, I was so excited about creating this revolutionary product. I knew I was creative, intuitive, and on point and that it was going to be exactly what the world needed. And as I predicted, it was a massive success.

After some powerful lessons and selling my interests in the company, I created and stepped into the work I do now. The law of compensation is never going to show up and give you more than what you believe you're worthy of. So, after a lot of restructuring and boundary setting, I got comfortable being uncomfortable, holding the line, and valuing myself on another level. I gained a level of trust and expansion that I never believed possible, which led to groundbreaking revolutions that I now pay forward.

It's always a struggle in the beginning, but you know when you're in the flow and nurturing with this law. When you are out of flow, you not only call it in, but you stop negotiating. Stay in your lane and stay out of other people's scarcity and money stories.

Now, the law of compensation isn't just about money, but the analogy I chose to use here was about self-worth, which, indeed, impacted my money. How many of you want more but negotiate with yourselves everywhere? This law requires you to present with integrity.

The good news is that I created a $1 million business, which I couldn't have held space for in the beginning. How did I do it? I did the work. I was willing to meet myself on a soul level and set the record straight. I was willing to call myself out on untrue stories. I was willing to invest in myself and spend the money. This eventually attracted enormous abundance as I no longer lived in the stories of the past but was thriving in the present.

There's no greater power than the law of compensation, but it will meet you only in the present moment. In fact, all of your power is in the present moment. It doesn't live in the past, and it certainly isn't in the future—but believe it or not, that's where most people live. Staying in the present moment is a superpower, and it's one that I'd like to teach you how to embrace.

When I started this journey of healing, I went to an event in Sedona. I really was there just to receive, and some of the biggest healers in the industry were in one room. Honestly, at the time, I wasn't even aware of who some of them were.

That five-day trip to Sedona changed my life. Not only did my energy in the room illuminate leaders, but I was stunned when I was recognized for my gifts and talent. They only knew me by my vibration—and isn't that what we're talking about here? Energy, vibration, where the law of compensation meets you. That changed the direction of the energy of my business. One of the questions I ask the most is how I attract and maintain the level of connections that I do. I am going to give it to you if you want to accept it or not. I trust the process and the fact that everything I am going to create is in the unknown. In the playfield of: I have no idea where this is coming from. I am married to the process and divorced from the outcome. And if you want to identify the maze, it will feel familiar as you play these stories over and over again, expecting a different outcome.

Every moment that you're awake, you're only one connection away from a miracle. If you show up and are seen, if you go into the arena, if you create, if you want to be courageous, you will get your ass kicked. That is guaranteed. As Brené Brown says, "If you're not in the arena getting your ass kicked, I'm not interested in your feedback."

So, if you're looking at changing your relationship to the law of compensation, you're going to need to go deeper. You're going to need to meet yourself in your vulnerability and shame. You're going to need to make friends with yourself. You're going to need to love and embrace every version of you.

I guarantee you that if I can do it, so can you. This is not the moment to armor up. This is the time to take off the armor, step up, claim it with your knees shaking, and know you're worth it.

If I have said it in this book already, I'm going to say it again here: there's only one you, and the world is waiting for your genius. The Latins believe that we all have a genius, but I believe that our superpower and genius coming together will illuminate the law of compensation, bringing in great abundance.

My question for you now is, what's stopping you from loving every version of yourself? You should be grateful for everything that brought you here.

THE LIE: *The push. The force. Not trusting the flow: work harder, push harder. You have to make a plan and stick to it. We have to work harder than the universe.*

THE TRUTH: *Your soul is on a mission. You will attract through nurture and flow. The universe has no limits.*

The law of compensation is a powerful universal principle that emphasizes the balance of giving and receiving. It teaches us that the value we provide to others directly correlates with what we receive in return. Abundance is not something we acquire, it's something we tune in to. In the words of Wayne Dyer, *"Abundance is not something we acquire. It is something we tune into."*

This law is about the ebb and flow of life, where the right actions are rewarded, promoting a harmonious balance. It is crucial to understand that compensation is always fair, but its vibrational match reflects what we give to the world. Do you see the conflict with my story? In exploring this law, we must delve into how we show up in the world.

We have to reflect on our internal beliefs and motives regarding compensation. Remember, compensation is never external. It is always an internal process.

It is so critical to understand what is compelling us forward, what we're connecting to, and why we are doing it. Where are you negotiating? What are you tolerating? Only you know. The world functions much like a multiplication table. What you put in will be what's returned to you. So says the law of compensation.

If we contribute positively, we can expect positive returns, shouldn't we? Certainly, because the law of compensation can be a complex and sensitive topic, especially in the context of personal relationships and experiences of infidelity.

The principle of balance here is that the law of compensation operates on the principle that the universe seeks balance. This means that every action has a corresponding reaction, and the energy we put into the world influences what we receive. However, this doesn't imply that every outcome is directly proportionate to the actions taken, particularly in interpersonal relationships.

My law of compensation was that I was a giver, but I had a very difficult time receiving. Let's recognize personal values. When people say you don't deserve something, it reflects a common belief that loyalty and commitment should yield trust and fidelity in return. While this is a reasonable explanation, and I certainly expected it, the reality is that other individuals may not always act in alignment with the values that I uphold.

The law of compensation reminds us that our worth is inherent, not determined by the actions of others. My faithfulness and love are valuable contributions to the relationship, and they reflect on my integrity and character, not on my partner's actions. These qualities contribute to the positive energy that I continue to carry forward, regardless of the actions that took place.

Now let's discuss the role of personal responsibility. Louise Hay's *Mirror Work* was the first book I picked up on self-love. After reading it, I recognized that to be loved and honored, I had to love and honor myself, and I hadn't even begun that journey yet.

The transformational power of adversity can be profoundly painful, but it can also catalyze growth and transformation. It can be like rocket fuel to the law of compensation, which suggests that every painful experience can lead to a valuable lesson and insight. Adversity can prompt us to reconnect with our inner selves, reassess priorities, and cultivate a deeper understanding of a love and trust that we may have never established otherwise.

I would not be who I am today without this experience. I'm not angry; I am deeply connected to self-love, acceptance, and forgiveness.

Ultimately, the law of compensation encourages healing and forgiveness. This process allows you to reclaim your power and recognize the power that you've never even taken. The balance of the universe may not always seem fair, but it operates on a larger scale, allowing for the unfolding of experiences that can lead you to a more aligned and fulfilled life.

I want to emphasize that while the universe seeks balance, it does not always manifest itself in straightforward or immediate ways. My commitment values didn't mean I was perfect in any way, but they contribute to my growth and understanding of love and relationships to this day.

I don't shame myself for not knowing what I wasn't supposed to know. Universal law claims that when we know better, we do better. The little girl inside of me couldn't have possibly had the tools to take on more than she did. She was so busy surviving, calling in, and dealing with chaos that she couldn't have possibly evolved to the level that I needed her to be at.

When I was ready and claimed the healing, my universe opened up. My connection with God, which I thought I had lost, returned. The gifts that I had been given as a young girl lit up like a Christmas tree. All of my unique, funky ways of doing things no longer embarrassed me. Instead, I embraced and celebrated them. Did it take me the full 60 years to arrive here? I haven't even arrived yet. When you commit to being a student of the universe, you're in it for the long haul.

I now understand on a much larger scale why things took place and why they played out like they did. I encourage you to reflect on your own experiences and the lessons learned. Even amidst pain and betrayal, there is potential for transformation and even resilience and, ultimately, a more empowered path forward.

Through this new lens, the law of compensation can be seen not just as a mechanism of balance but also as a guide for personal growth and healing. From my story, you can see that the law of compensation was very active in me regaining balance in my personal life. If you are ready, I want to invite you to unpack your beliefs and motives.

Compensation is never external; it's always internal. It's an inside job, and it asks you, "What do you need? What do you desire? Where are you afraid?" What you put in will be returned, but again, I want to anchor you in what you're receiving.

You may be stuck in a loop that you haven't identified yet. Maybe you haven't put in the work yet, and you don't yet understand why you call in things like betrayal. This is where you might want to embrace the law of sacrifice and process it as a pathway to success. Ask yourself, "What am I willing to give up?" Perhaps there's something that's been protecting you that you're willing to sacrifice to activate this law, which means feeling all the feels.

Yes, it hurt. There were times I didn't think I was going to be able to breathe. Betrayal is a horrible, horrible emotion.

Many people don't overcome it. However, by using this universal law, I not only guarantee that you will, but if you embrace your truth and get past the violation, your life will expand exponentially. It is so essential to intertwine it with the law of cause and effect and the law of attraction because each of these laws supports and amplifies the others.

The law of cause and effect tells us that every action has a reaction. If we take a positive action, we can create a chain of effect that leads to favorable outcomes. The law of attraction emphasizes that like attracts like, and our beliefs and thoughts shape our reality. Embracing these laws collectively enables us to understand that our stories must be aligned with our intentions. If our internal narrative doesn't match our desired outcomes, we may struggle to manifest what we truly want.

It's important to address the lies we often tell ourselves about the law of compensation. One common misconception is that it is solely about sacrifice. Many believe that to receive, they must give up something significant or endure hardship. However, the truth is that the process of giving and receiving can be joyful and enriching.

Another lie is that compensation is external, that our worth is determined by what others think about us or how they respond to us. The reality is that true compensation comes from within. It is about self-worth and recognizing the value we bring to the world.

To use the law of compensation in your daily life, consider these simple steps. The first is self-reflection. Regularly reflect on how you show up in the world. What actions are you taking? What energies are you projecting?

Journaling can be an effective tool in self-exploration. Identify limited beliefs. Unpack the stories you tell yourself regarding compensation. Are there beliefs holding you back from receiving what you desire? Challenge these beliefs and replace them with empowering thoughts.

Embrace the balance, recognizing that the natural spiritual balance is in everything. Giving and receiving are two sides of the same coin. Make a conscious decision to be generous and openhearted, and understand that this generosity will return to you in kind. Forgiveness is expansion. Forgiveness does not lie in the ego energy, which protects, shuts down, judges, and divides.

Next, commit to change. If you desire a different outcome, you have to commit to making changes in your actions and mindset. This commitment is not just about doing things differently; it's about cultivating a new way of being that aligns with your values.

I had to destroy my life to reconstruct a new structure and use this law of compensation because, for the little girl who needed safety, I built the safety within. She no longer needs that in the external world because she now gets that from me. Now I can show up and have a new relationship.

Practice gratitude. Cultivating a sense of gratitude for where you've been and the contributions you've made. This practice reinforces the understanding that what you give is valuable and appreciated.

Remain open to receiving. This may involve overcoming fears of insecurity about your worthiness. I want you to affirm the right to receive good things in your life. Say, "I deserve. I want. I desire." I also want you to affirm your right to receive good things in your life. You may subconsciously not believe that you're worthy of that. That's why using these tools is so important.

The law of compensation operates within the framework of a natural spiritual balance, the highs and lows of where you move. This balance is not a one-size-fits-all approach—each person's journey is unique. Not everyone will be affected by infidelity, but by recognizing your patterns and beliefs, you can navigate your path more effectively.

Consider your double binds around this law. What stories are you telling yourself? What is your belief system regarding your worth and what you're giving and receiving? Addressing these questions can help you break free from limiting patterns and embrace a more abundant mindset.

If we're looking at the law of compensation, we are looking to receive more. We are looking for harmony and balance in the universe. Embracing this journey and activating the law of compensation invites us to reflect on the connectedness of all of our actions and the outcomes that we've experienced. By understanding this law in conjunction with the law of cause and effect and the law of attraction, we can cultivate a life that is rich, meaningful, and fulfilling.

Embrace the process as a pathway to success. Recognize that every contribution you make has the potential to return in ways that enhance your life immeasurably. Ultimately, this journey towards understanding and applying the law of compensation is also about recognizing your inherent value and the impact you have on the world, that we are all interconnected. As you align your beliefs with your actions and remain open to the flow of giving and receiving, you create a harmonious existence that reflects the beauty of this universal law.

As we continue to explore the law of compensation, it's essential to intertwine it with cause and effect and the law of attraction because each law supports and amplifies the other. Embracing these laws collectively enables us to understand that our stories must be aligned with our intentions.

If our internal narrative does not match our desired outcome, we may struggle to manifest what we truly want, and we'll be constantly out of alignment.

To apply compensation in your daily life, I want you to consider these steps. The first is self-reflection. Reflect on how you're showing up in the world. What energies are you protecting or approaching? Journaling is a really beautiful and effective tool for this self-exploration.

Identify your limiting beliefs. Look at the stories related to how you are receiving compensation in the world. What could be holding you back? I want you to challenge these beliefs and replace them with empowering thoughts. Embrace the balance, recognizing that there is balance in everything.

Giving and receiving are two sides of the coin. What coin are you flipping, and where does it land in your life? I want you to commit to change. If you desire a different outcome, commit to making the changes in your actions and mindset. And this is never a one-and-done. This commitment is about doing things differently and cultivating a new way of being that aligns with your values.

Always practice gratitude. There's nothing higher vibrationally than allowing your relationship with gratitude to manifest and be appreciated, reinforcing where your contributions are in the world.

Stay open to receiving. The law of compensation means we must be open to receiving. The left-hand side of our body is the feminine, receiving side, and we must have the ebb and flow of this. The balance must be here, the natural spiritual balance.

Are you in balance here? You might want to look at the balance of your physical body and your physical ailments. I often had many injuries on the left side of my body, and when I was out of balance, they appeared on the right side, too.

Have you experienced injuries on one side of the body or the other? Were they on your feminine side or your masculine side? Can you identify where you show up more in your life than that? I want you to consider your double binds around this law.

What stories are you telling yourself? What is your belief system regarding your worth? Cause and effect sets all the other universal laws in motion. Ultimately, this law will be recognized in your value system and the impact that you choose to have on the world.

What can you do to apply the data right now? You can reflect on how you can shift your attitude and mindset. You can start with micro-level changes in your daily approach. You can acknowledge and value the work you put in as a step toward greater compensation.

You can cultivate a positive internal dialogue and break cycles of negativity or complaining. Understanding this law can help you activate the law of compensation and redirect your energies, actions, and mindset. It also reinforces the idea that change starts from within and reflects outwardly.

Everything is an inside job. If you don't feel you're receiving what you deserve, you may be stuck in a loop of complaint negativity. That loop is a story you've created.

As we've discussed, 95% of the subconscious is running the show. So, we need to activate this law with clear, clean authority, which means showing up with authority in your life. You have the power to change your situation by changing your mindset. The more work you do internally, the better value your output will have and the more compensation you will receive.

QUESTIONS FOR REFLECTION

Where are you negotiating?

_____

_____

_____

Are there beliefs holding you back from receiving what you desire?

_____

_____

_____

What is your belief system regarding your worth and what you're giving and receiving?

_____

_____

_____

THE TRUTH WITHIN THE LIE

What energies are you protecting or approaching?

_____

_____

_____

What stories are you telling yourself?

_____

_____

_____

What is your belief system regarding your worth?

_____

_____

_____

CHAPTER 9
ARE YOU READY TO LET GO?
THE LAW OF SACRIFICE

*"Sometimes you have to let go of the life you planned
to embrace the life that is waiting for you."*
~ Joseph Campbell

Worry, fear, and doubt often serve as barriers that keep us entrenched in the struggle. These emotions can not only feel overwhelming, but they can also lead us to believe that they are integral in our nature. However, they are often learned responses, and they are deeply rooted in our subconscious rather than reflections of our true selves.

By understanding the law of sacrifice, we can begin to make conscious choices to let go of what no longer serves us, creating space for growth, healing, and abundance.

Sacrifice is not merely about loss. It's about transformation. When we sacrifice worry, fear, and doubt, we make room for clarity, confidence, and faith. It invites us to ask ourselves critical questions. What is the actual problem we need to solve? What is our biggest challenge? These inquiries encourage us to step into vulnerability, recognizing that moving forward in faith often requires us to confront our fears and rewire our thought patterns.

Shifting our perspective about this allows us to embrace the trust and abundance that is our birthright. A powerful shift in perspective can not only change the way we navigate our life's challenges but also serve as a reminder that divine goodness and abundance are always available to us. When we adopt the belief that nothing worthy of God is unworthy of us, we begin to understand our inherent value and the importance of nurturing a mindset of abundance.

It also steps us out of judgment in our own stories. In fact, the law of sacrifice played a pivotal role in my transformation. This sacrifice wasn't just about food; it represented a commitment to nourishing my body and making healthier choices.

You might ask how I gained 90 pounds in two years. The answer is not a simple one, but I'm going to give it to you straight. I psychologically surrendered. My metabolism shut down. I got very still. Was it years of having an eating disorder and perfection paralysis that got me there? Did I need to go there to love myself at a level that I had never experienced? Perhaps. I'm still working that one out.

That was my process, and I've never criticized myself for it. Did I like it? No, but I embraced it. I even bought Gucci belts that fit me at that size. I was healing and loving myself at a different level, and if I needed to go there, then that's what my soul did.

It took me a year to lose the weight. It was the first time that I didn't want to lose weight to be skinny. I wanted to get healthy. That's what I chose, and that's what I'll choose for the rest of my life. The pendulum that swung for many years has stopped. I had to choose something that was a higher vibration that I could align with, and that could support my being skinny. Shaming myself wasn't going to cut it at this time.

Surrender can be your best friend. I surrendered all those versions of myself and used the law of sacrifice to no longer beat myself up and shame myself. I sacrificed all of that to find a love for myself that is eternal. I had to sacrifice the version of me, the skinny woman, to love the whole woman

---

THE LIE: *I had to be perfect to be accepted and loved.*

THE TRUTH: *Loving myself is where I met myself. That feeling is better than perfection.*

Perfection paralysis will tie you up like Gumby. There is no such thing as perfection. There is only what you do and don't do. All your power lies in the choices available to you. The truth is that you have to make space. You must sacrifice the current version of yourself to make space for the one you haven't met yet.

At that point in my life, being healthy was the only thing I focused on. This allowed me to commit to my body and make healthier choices. It no longer became about losing weight. It became about sacrificing the pain and trauma. Every day, we get to choose what we want in this life. If I had stayed on that hamster wheel of perfectionism, I would never have committed to losing the weight.

I had to use the law of sacrifice to give up the pain that I was taking ownership of. Moreover, I had to confront my lifelong reactivity. Growing up in a reactive environment with a father who struggled with alcoholism and an emotionally unavailable mother, I learned to react rather than respond.

The absence of nurturing and flow in my upbringing shaped my emotional patterns. I had to give up the false image. I had to take off my rose-colored glasses and face the pain and the truth of their imperfections. I had to sacrifice their approval to find myself.

I realized the need to sacrifice the reactivity that had defined me for so long. I had to get radically honest with myself, and I had to shed the stories that I had constructed, not only to survive but to embrace the truth of all my experiences without judgment. If we judge, we're back on the hamster wheel.

Through this process, the healing began, allowing me to close the gap of unresolved emotions and unprocessed trauma from my childhood so I could start the process of healing myself.

This is what is required to cultivate a life of flow, nurturing, and abundance. We must be willing to identify and relinquish what no longer serves us, and this involves radical honesty, confronting the narratives that we tell ourselves, and acknowledging their origins.

This honesty creates a foundation for genuine healing. The pendulum will swing back and forth. You often see this in someone's life, whether it be addiction, being overweight, gambling, etc. They are desperately trying to avoid the pain using coping mechanisms that immediately numb but never heal.

If we do not commit to true healing and use the law of sacrifice, giving up the vices and the emotional anchoring that we are devoted to, we cannot create the necessary space and momentum in the balance of sacrifice. We need to make conscious choices. We have to identify that we are willing to sacrifice, whether it be reactive behavior, unhealthy habits, or limiting beliefs.

The law of sacrifice requires us to give up something to receive the gifts of healing and abundance. This law works with the law of abundance. It makes space for abundance. Without using the law of sacrifice, we do not have room for abundance.

As we engage with the law of sacrifice and explore the interplay between the feminine and the masculine energies, we want to recognize that embracing the feminine energy of nurturing and receptivity allows us to create a balanced approach to life. This shift requires us to let go of rigid and often overly masculine energy of control, sometimes forcefulness, and make space for softness and acceptance.

The law of sacrifice invites us to embark on a journey of healing by letting go of what no longer serves us. By sacrificing worry, fear, and doubt, we create an opening for clarity, trust, and abundance.

This journey is not without its challenges, but through honesty and self-awareness, we can rewrite our stories and cultivate the light that reflects our truth.

The law of sacrifice also requires us to feel it all, the good and the bad. There is no judgment here. There's only what we do and what we don't do.

As we continue to explore the law of sacrifice, I want you to embrace the transformation that the power of this law holds. You wouldn't think that giving up things would create such clarity, but it does. By making conscious choices and recognizing the value of what we're willing to release, we can step into an unimaginable life.

Often, we've used armor to protect ourselves from feeling—even from feeling abundance. We may not have a relationship with it yet. So, as we learn to explore the law of sacrifice, we want to uncover and lean into the depth of this law and its profound impacts on our lives.

The universal law of sacrifice posits that to achieve our desires, we must be willing to give up something of value. This law operates on the principle that every action has a cost and that the universe often requires a form of exchange to manifest our intentions. Whether it's time, resources, relationships, or certain beliefs, what we sacrifice plays a crucial role in our personal growth and the attainment of our goals.

Sacrifice does not imply loss or deprivation. Rather, it is an investment in our future selves. By letting go of what no longer serves us, we create a space for new opportunities and growth. This is the only law that allows us to do that. This could mean sacrificing comfort for the sake of pursuing a passion or relinquishing unhealthy habits to embrace a healthier lifestyle.

I had to relinquish late-night eating, but that wasn't enough. My playing field was full of pain and deregulation, so I had to give up the violation, betrayal, and hurt to embrace the healing.

To embrace weight loss, I had to use the law of sacrifice. I had to give up the pain that I wrapped myself in as my armor. I was needing everyone to know how much pain was being inflicted on me because I was in victim mode.

Identifying that we are in victim mode means that we have to start reflecting on our current circumstances and identifying what we're willing to sacrifice and what change is necessary. What habits, beliefs, or commitments are preventing you from moving forward? Consider what you're willing to let go of right now to make room for what you desire. What is on the back burner? What is it that you have always wanted to do, but something is in its way and preventing it? What can you give up to embrace and explore what that looks like?

Try to understand that sacrifice often involves discomfort. Recognizing that every sacrifice made is a step towards achieving your dreams. You will not know the outcome, but knowing that you're sacrificing and claiming your dreams cultivates the resilience you need to create abundance in your life.

The universe responds to our sacrifices by opening doors to new opportunities. When you sacrifice out of a genuine desire to grow without manipulation, you align yourself with a flow of abundance. Sacrifice fosters growth and self-discovery, allowing us to evolve and reach our potential.

Commitment to the law of sacrifice means sacrificing something that is of value to you. This creates a ripple effect, attracting positive outcomes and opportunities in your life and creating the space that you've needed to build out the life you desire.

Now, sometimes, people think sacrifice means loss. The idea of sacrifice can evoke fear, making it a challenge for a lot of us to let go of what we hold dear. What would life look like if we let go of everything comfortable?

Some may misconstrue sacrifice as a negative experience, leading to feelings of resentment and regret. This is a story they've created so they don't have to be uncomfortable. However, the universal law of sacrifice is about recognizing and embracing the necessary changes that life demands for our growth and success.

By understanding what we need to sacrifice and how to navigate the discomfort that comes with it, we can not only harness this law to transform our lives, but we can embrace it as the most powerful tool in our journey to date. We can watch as the universe responds to our commitment with opportunities and abundance.

This is the essence of sacrifice. At its core, sacrifice is a transformational process.

It not only invites us to evaluate our priorities, but it helps us make conscious choices about what truly matters. This evolution often leads to profound insights into our core values and desires. For instance, some may realize that pursuing a higher salary at the expense of their health is not a worthwhile trade-off, prompting a shift in their career path.

Sacrifice can also serve as a means of emotional release. Letting go of toxic relationships, old habits, or limiting beliefs can clear mental and emotional space for new experiences. This release allows us to move forward unencumbered, fostering a sense of freedom and possibility.

Sacrifice can also create a ripple effect. Making a significant sacrifice can inspire others to evaluate their lives and make a change. This communal aspect of sacrifice can lead to collective growth and upliftment, creating a supportive environment for everyone. Where in your life can you see the ripple effect of your decisions?

In applying the law of sacrifice, we want to set intentions. These can be related not only to personal development but to career goals, relationships, or anything else you want in your life. Once you have clarity on your intentions, you can identify what you may need to sacrifice to achieve them. This could be dedicating time to study, letting go of unproductive relationships, or investing money in a course. Develop a plan that outlines the specific sacrifices you are willing to make.

If you're not willing to sacrifice, you're going to continue to spin in the same circumstances. But if you use the sacrifice plan—this can include daily routines, time management, lifestyle changes, and writing down your intentions—it can help solidify your commitment and serve as a reminder during challenging times of what you are willing to give up to achieve your goal.

Write down what you're willing to claim and keep it somewhere that you can see it. Practicing mindfulness supports this, so cultivate mindfulness to help you navigate the emotional aspects of sacrifice.

Recognizing fear, doubt, and resistance can empower you to move through them rather than be paralyzed by them. Worry, doubt, and fear keep you in the bind. They keep you in the loop. However, mindful practices, such as meditation or journaling, can help you not only navigate your emotions but also maintain focus on your goals.

Don't forget to celebrate the small wins. Recognizing even the smallest achievements can boost your motivation and reinforce your commitment to your goals. This practice can also help you balance the emotional weight of sacrifice and positive reinforcement.

Negotiating with yourself is a very productive way to apply the law of sacrifice. I had a client with temporomandibular joint disorder (TMJ). She loved chewing gum, but it created an enormous pain in her jaw. She realized that she had to sacrifice her love for gum to heal her TMJ. So, she negotiated with herself. She gave up the gum, replacing it with mints, and healed her jaw.

When using the law of sacrifice, we balance out by calling in what we need with the law of attraction. When you sacrifice something valuable, you signify to the universe your commitment to attracting something greater. This alignment creates a powerful energy that draws opportunities and resources into your life. This takes minimal effort, but it does take maximum focus.

Sacrifice also embodies the principles of cause and effect. Every choice has a consequence. By consciously choosing to sacrifice, you actively shape the outcome of your life. This understanding encourages responsibility and empowers you to take control of your destiny. Nothing is random in the universe.

Sacrifice also relates to the law of vibration. When your thoughts and actions emit frequencies that resonate with similar energies, when you sacrifice for your goals, you're elevating your vibration and aligning yourself with higher frequencies that attract positive experiences. You're not tripping into circumstances. You are curating and designing.

One of the pros of sacrifice is empowerment. Sacrifice empowers you to take charge of your life and make conscious choices that align with what you truly desire. It's a dance of all the universal laws together.

Sacrifice also builds resilience and mental strength and prepares you for future challenges. It also helps clarify priorities, enabling you to focus on what truly matters.

One of the cons is that there's a risk of over-sacrificing to the point of burnout or neglecting self-care. It's crucial to maintain balance to ensure that sacrifices do not compromise your well-being.

Sometimes, people may sacrifice the wrong things, such as their health or happiness, in pursuit of external validation. It's vital not only to identify but to evaluate the value of what you are sacrificing carefully. Assess, make a list, and ask yourself, "How is this serving my higher self?"

The universal law of sacrifice is not only a profound principle, but it also invites you to make intentional choices for your growth and fulfillment. By understanding the nuances of what it means to sacrifice and your relationship to it, you can leverage this law to transform your life positively.

Embracing the path of sacrifice is not only a pathway to greater clarity, abundance, and personal empowerment, but it also allows you to witness how the universe responds to your commitment with opportunities and abundance. It is such a compelling law that I really want you to reflect on what you can give up to claim what you truly want.

The law of sacrifice is an everyday application. Think about it as time management. One of the most valuable resources we have is time, and you might be sacrificing too much of it on unproductive activities like social media or television.

Instead, allocate that time to personal growth, such as learning a new skill, exercising, or pursuing a passion project. This conscious redirection can lead to significant personal development and fulfillment.

So, I'm going to ask you again: What can you sacrifice today? Some might choose to wake up an hour earlier each day to meditate or read, sacrificing extra sleep for mental clarity and knowledge.

I wake up every day at 3:00 a.m. For the next hour, my vibrational energy to meditate is at its highest. This allows me to connect on a deeper, more spiritual level, and I am committed to that. So, I sacrifice an hour of sleep, and I sacrifice staying up an extra hour. Sometimes, I sacrifice my sleep, but this higher vibration is worth it.

Sacrificing immediate pleasure for long-term financial goals can also be a powerful application of this law. This might mean forgoing expensive dining out and luxurious hotels.

I'm not saying to sacrifice all of your luxuries, but to save for investments, a house, or education, you must sacrifice some of the things that you have enjoyed. This approach not only fosters a mindset of abundance but also prioritizes future gains over temporary satisfaction.

Temporary satisfaction will not give you long-term abundance. You must use the law of sacrifice here, look at your life, and assess it truthfully. Make a list of what you can sacrifice so you can attain what it is that has eluded you up until this point.

For example, a young, professional person might decide to live with roommates to save money, sacrificing personal space for the ability to invest in a course that enhances their career or completes their degree.

Next, I want to look at the emotional boundaries of using the law of sacrifice. Sometimes, sacrifice involves letting go of relationships or commitments that drain your energy. This can be a profound act of self-care. By prioritizing your emotional well-being, you create a space for healthy relationships and opportunities that align with your authentic self.

Once again, we must claim our truth. To lose the weight that I did, I had to sacrifice a toxic, unhealthy relationship that no longer served me. It was not easy to sacrifice this, but I was committed to my health. This left me not only losing 90 pounds but also in an excellent space emotionally because I chose to distance myself from toxic relationships. I had to sacrifice past connections to foster a more supportive social circle. I had to vibrate at a different level to attract what I needed.

Sacrifice leads to improved concentration on your goals. You create time and space, and when you let go of distractions, you can devote more energy and attention to what truly matters.

Embracing discomfort with no shame not only builds your resilience but allows you to navigate challenges and foster a mindset that sees obstacles as opportunities for learning and evolution. There are no mistakes here. There's only a process of ebb and flow, release and gain.

We must sacrifice to align with our core values. So, write down one core value that will lead to a more authentic life. If you're going to use the law of sacrifice, you're going to want to claim not only your authentic life but your core values as well.

This alignment creates a sense of fulfillment. Making sacrifices not only feels meaningful but also releases burdensome things. We need to create space for abundance.

It's like a cha-cha-cha, the law of abundance and the law of sacrifice. We can't have abundance without using the law of sacrifice. By sacrificing what no longer serves you, you open yourself up to receiving anything and everything that you want—and it can come in rather quickly.

I'm going to say it again: by sacrificing what no longer serves you, you open yourself up to receiving new opportunities, and this is where the law of abundance comes into play.

The act of letting go creates a vacuum that the universe will fill with unimaginable wealth, opportunities that you cannot comprehend, and experiences that will make you think, *"How in the world did I create this?"* Well, you created the space just by activating the law of sacrifice, which has connected you with the law of abundance.

The law of sacrifice and the law of abundance work in tandem. The law of abundance posits that there's an infinite supply of resources, opportunities, and wealth available. This suggests that when we align our thoughts, actions, and sacrifices with our desires, we can tap into unimaginable abundance.

By sacrificing something of lesser value, you signal to the universe your readiness to receive greater abundance. This exchange is reciprocal. The universe responds to your commitment to providing opportunities that resonate with your sacrifice.

Remember, you have to be committed to your commitment, so be very clear on what you're committed to. Whatever it is, you will receive it.

If someone sacrifices their time and energy to volunteer for a cause they care about, they may find that they attract new connections, new resources, or even unexpected job offers that align with their passions. I have seen this in my coaching practice over and over again.

Think outside the box and use your unique perspective on sacrifice. Use it as a creative force. Sacrifice can actually inspire creativity. When faced with limitations, you can tap into the creative potential to find solutions. This can lead to innovative ideas and approaches that wouldn't have emerged otherwise.

So, as you can see, sacrificing is the foundation for calling anything in. For example, a startup founder might sacrifice a comfortable salary to pursue their passion for entrepreneurship. This sacrifice can foster innovative thinking as they navigate the challenges of building a business, leading to creative solutions that set them apart in the market.

Next, let's look at sacrifice and spiritual growth. How are they connected? Many spiritual traditions emphasize sacrifice as a path to enlightenment or a deeper connection with the divine. This concept encourages us to view sacrifices as part of a larger spiritual journey, fostering a sense of purpose and interconnectedness. For example, engaging in acts of service can be seen as a spiritual sacrifice that not only benefits others but enriches the giver's life with a sense of fulfillment and connection.

Understanding that sacrifice is often cyclical can also shift one's perspective. Sacrifices made in one area may lead to abundance in another, creating a dynamic flow of give and take. This cyclical understanding encourages a mindset of trust in the process and life.

For example, a teacher who sacrifices personal time to mentor a student may find that the relationship built during that time leads to unexpected career opportunities or collaborations later on. Again, I see this in my coaching practice on a daily basis.

Sacrifice can be used in every aspect of your life, from time management to emotional well-being. By embracing the discomfort that comes with sacrifice and recognizing its connection to the law of abundance, we can create a life filled with purpose, growth, and unimaginable opportunity. Whether through small daily choices or significant life decisions, understanding and working with the law of sacrifice can transform challenges into opportunities for abundance and fulfillment.

If you have not recognized the value at this point, and if you are not willing to let go and make room for the blessings that the universe has to offer, I'm going to ask you right now: What are you waiting for? Time is finite.

I want you to look at your relationship to what you have sacrificed up until this point. Have you explored the nuances, practical application, and broader implications of how it can impact not only your growth but also the people in your life? What would it look like if you used the law of sacrifice at this level and at this time of your life? There is no right or wrong. There is only when you choose to activate and use it.

So, call it in. Use it. And again, there is no secret sauce. There is nothing that you need to do to prepare yourself. There's only claiming the law of sacrifice and realizing what it is you need to release. The act of sacrifice is a conscious choice. You must choose to sacrifice something.

When you do, you align your actions with your values, reducing the dissonance. This alignment fosters a sense of integrity and authenticity that vibrates at the highest level, calling in everything you desire.

Here's another example. Someone who values health may sacrifice late-night outings with friends to prioritize sleep and exercise. This decision aligns their actions with their core values, leading to greater overall satisfaction and well-being. This is exactly what I did.

I sacrificed late-night eating. I sacrificed everything that I was putting into play to align with my core values and prioritize my health, which meant more sleep, more exercise, eating earlier, and planning meals. It was a process. By using the law of sacrifice, I created the space not only for health but for the unimaginable wealth that came with it because my vibration was raised exponentially.

I want you to look at this as empowerment through your choice. Your greatest power is the right to choose, and sacrifice is fundamentally a choice. Embrace the power of choice and look at how it can transform the experience of sacrificing from one of loss to one of empowerment. Don't look at it as having to give something up. Instead, look at it as an opportunity to gain.

Sacrifice is working for you, not against you. When you view sacrifices as conscious decisions made for our growth, you regain control over your life, which puts you on a path of divine intervention.

As we do this, we actually build emotional resilience. The emotional challenges that come with sacrifice can not only lead to emotional resilience, but by facing this discomfort and learning to cope with it, we develop an ability to navigate with greater ease. This emotional fortitude can enhance our overall well-being in every area of our lives.

I want to give you some tools to embrace the law of sacrifice. The first is to do reflective journaling. Write down and explore your feelings about sacrifice. Write about what you're willing to give up, how you feel about it, and what you hope to gain, and clarify your intentions and strengthen your resolve.

Next, I want you to practice mindful awareness. By doing this, you become more aware of your thoughts and feelings regarding sacrifice. You become mindful, not mindless. Using techniques that assist you in processing emotions, reducing anxiety, and fostering acceptance of the sacrifices that you choose to make on a daily basis is so rewarding.

With that comes goal setting with sacrifice in mind. When setting your personal and professional goals, identify the sacrifices that you may need to make to achieve them. Are you willing to accept these sacrifices? You can mentally prepare yourself, making the transition smoother.

I also want to encourage you to cultivate a sense of community, as it can enhance the experience of sacrifice. Engaging with people who share similar goals or values can provide support and motivation. This collective approach can transform what you're sacrificing into shared experiences that create deeper connections of understanding.

On a societal level, sacrifice can lead to cultural shifts. Prioritizing collective well-being over individual gain can create environments that foster collaboration and support. What would your life look like with this collective approach, and how can it lead to greater harmony and resilience in your personal life? How can you create a more sustainable future by using the law of sacrifice?

Claiming your personal relationship to the law of sacrifice can lead to new passion, interest, and self-awareness. It opens up doors and connects you to a higher purpose that you may not even claim yet because you are not aware that it's available to you. Many artists use sacrifice in their process. They're willing to sacrifice comfort, stability, or even relationships for the sake of their art.

Cultivating gratitude can be a powerful way to embrace the sacrifices we make by focusing on what we gain from our sacrifices rather than what we've lost. We shift our mindset from scarcity to abundance. This practice enhances our sense of fulfillment and happiness.

Healthy relationships often involve sacrifice. Partners may choose to forego personal desires for the sake of the relationship's well-being. Have you ever experienced that in your life? Understanding this dynamic can foster empathy and strengthen bonds, but as an individual, you can recognize that sacrifices made in love contribute to the relationship's growth. This, in turn, contributes to your growth and expansion.

The universal law of sacrifice is a profound and multifaceted principle that can significantly impact personal growth, relationships, community, and well-being. There are no limits here. By understanding how you can consciously embrace sacrifice, you can not only transform your life, but you can cultivate resilience and tap into the abundance that follows.

I encourage you to look at the broader implications of sacrifice, not only with regard to cultural shifts but to environmental stewardship, and how, by creating more space in your life, you create a larger perspective that deepens your gratitude. This allows you to view sacrifice not as a burden but as a powerful catalyst for transformation, forging a deeper connection between yourself and the world around you.

I had to give up my old belief system piece by piece. I had to sacrifice my old story to create my new life. I had to release my old patterns and thoughts to find safety within. If I hadn't, I would have continued to self-abandon. I had to trust that my home was within me, not in the external world.

The law of sacrifice allowed me to do the work to hold myself and my inner child and let her know that we were safe. But I had to give up the lie that I was not safe and could not change. The truth is, in every moment of every day, choice is our greatest power.

I had the right to choose a new story that I wasn't destined to live in an abandoned world, that I could choose to hold space for myself. The truth was that self-love was available to me. I just had not been exposed to that story yet.

You can achieve anything in your life with the law of sacrifice. What is it you're willing to give up? Martin Luther King Jr. said that you can't achieve anything in your life without a small amount of sacrifice. I believe that sacrifice is necessary to move forward and make room for new stories.

Sacrificing old thoughts, even though they provide safety, is key. Maybe now they aren't safe, and you're recognizing the pattern that is spinning you. The mindset that brought you here cannot take you further.

Sacrifice involves letting go to receive something greater. Think of it this way: trees release their leaves every season. Old leaves fall to make room for the new growth in spring. Visualize that. They don't mourn. They just release. It's a process. So, keep your hands and heart open and recognize that sacrifice doesn't have to be a negative thing. It means expansion. It means that you get to choose. It means celebration.

THE TRUTH WITHIN THE LIE

Are you willing to sacrifice something protective to achieve what you want? Are you willing to release it to create something that may not feel safe?

Sacrifice is about surrendering what you know to trust and what your evolution may look like. You can't predict what it feels like. That is where the terror barrier and fear come in. That's why people engulf themselves in old stories. So, give yourself the faith to trust and take a step forward. Know that you're connected to God.

Know that divine intervention is always with you and that you are not alone in this process. Know that the what-ifs often stem from ego, fear, and insecurity. Identify that. Your job is to be a master identifier. The ego will keep you in familiarity, and it wants to judge, protect, and contract.

The truth is that this law is simple yet deeply intimate. If you are willing to release something deeply rooted that often serves as armor, you allow yourself the freedom and expansion to live a life that you have not yet experienced.

So, if you want to create room for your true desires, remember that you have to sacrifice false protections for greater possibilities. Although they may have served a purpose, these false protections have held you back, and the time you have is finite.

Sacrifice leads to newness and expansion. This is connected to your heart energy, your feminine energy. To receive, we must release masculine energy.

When I started writing this book, I had only lost 75 pounds, and now I've lost 90. I've hit my goal. I set a goal, and I sacrificed ice cream at night, comfort food, and everything that I thought I deserved because I was going through extreme trauma and betrayal. I recognized that I was living a lie by justifying my treats as a reward for my hard work.

I was overworking. I didn't shame myself. I chose to make microchanges, not macro. I chose health and longevity. I didn't choose a specific number. Had I chosen 90 pounds, I probably wouldn't have made it.

I did it pound by pound. I chose health one step at a time because I knew that it was obtainable. I knew I could sacrifice the ice cream. I knew I could sacrifice to achieve. I knew I needed to plan out a little bit better. I couldn't just fall into each day. There were no excuses because I set my environment up for success.

The guiding question I want to leave you with is: Does sacrifice feel like love? If it doesn't, don't do it, because I guarantee you that sacrifice does feel like love. It does feel like support. It makes space for everything you need in your life.

What do you need? If you want more money, look at your finances. What are you willing to sacrifice? If you've got 19 streaming service subscriptions, do you need them all? If you want to put money away, consider how your routine is becoming a numbing prison. The biggest obstacle, my friends, is you.

Write down what you're willing to sacrifice. Write down what you want. List what you're willing to do to achieve your desires. Reflect on what you may be a slave to. Assess where your mindlessness is taking you. Determine where you're numbing out. Check if your actions are aligned and intentional and review daily your actions and intentions on a micro level. Do they feel like love? What are you willing to give up? Are you honoring yourself?

Lastly, look in the mirror every day and say, "What do I need from myself? Am I honoring myself? What am I willing to sacrifice to live the life that I would like to build?"

QUESTIONS FOR REFLECTION

What habits, beliefs, or commitments are preventing you from moving forward?

_____

_____

_____

What can you give up to embrace and explore what success looks like?

_____

_____

_____

What would life look like if you let go of everything comfortable?

_____

_____

_____

Where in your life can you see the ripple effect of your decisions?

_____

_____

_____

What can you sacrifice today?

_____

_____

_____

How can you create a more sustainable future by using the law of sacrifice?

_____

_____

_____

Are you honoring yourself?

_____

_____

_____

What are you willing to sacrifice to live the life that you would like to build?

_____

_____

_____

CHAPTER 10
CAN I BE CONNECTED TO BOTH?
LAW OF RELATIVITY

"We are all connected to each other, biologically, to the earth, chemically, to the stars, astronomically. I think we are all just a tiny little speck in the grand scheme of things."
~ Neil DeGrasse Tyson

For most of my life, I did not trust my intuition. This internal connection with the divine has allowed me to perceive things beyond the ordinary and sense truths that often go unseen. However, for many years, I struggled with self-doubt, second-guessing my decisions, and seeking validation from the external world.

Who was I to know anything? I had imposter syndrome, and I did not believe that God would actually give me this gift. There was a lot of internal conflict, and I failed to recognize the guidance within me, leaving me in peril and in a state of chaos most of the time.

THE LIE: *I couldn't be connected to anything holy and a seer, a knower. I am apprehensive about calling myself a psychic medium; I was just born with the gift of knowing.*

THE TRUTH: *This gift was a direct connection to the Source, to God, and the Universe. I was meant to embrace it and never second-guess it.*

Have you ever second-guessed yourself and wished you had gone with the first thought? Well, as I began to explore the law of relativity, I discovered how to use this understanding to reshape my narrative. This is a powerful law.

I learned that no matter how challenging my experiences were, they were essentially supporting my growth. This realization allowed me to drop deeper into the knowing that guides me every day. I now recognize that every moment, every choice, and every relationship exists in relation to something else. These principles have transformed my relationships with myself and the world around me, not only to the divine but to everyone and everything.

So, let's dive into the nature of the law of relativity.

This law teaches us that everything exists in relationship to something else and our experience is not isolated. How many of you feel isolated in your decisions and disconnected from the source and the world? They are interconnected with and influenced by various factors, including our perceptions, our beliefs, and the environment we inhabit.

What's significant for one person may not hold the same weight in truth for another. For example, a setback that feels devastating for one person might be perceived as an opportunity for growth by another. This relativity allows us to appreciate the diversity of human experience, and it fosters empathy for others.

Conceptual understanding is the context in which we experience life, and it shapes our interpretations and reactions. By recognizing that external circumstances influence our feelings and thoughts, we can cultivate a more adaptable mindset. We are not isolated in our world. This understanding empowers us not only to view our experiences through a lens of relativity but also helps us navigate challenges with greater resilience.

When we view obstacles as opportunities, we transform our relationship with adversity. Have you ever considered approaching adversity without resistance but with acceptance? To do this, we must reframe failure.

Instead of perceiving failure as a definition or a definitive endpoint, we must see it as a vital part of our journey. There is no failure. Each setback carries lessons that contribute to our evolution.

For instance, I learned to embrace my past choices—those that I once labeled as mistakes—and even shamed myself for. That shame allows us to stay in the shadow work where we never embrace the law of relativity.

Recognizing the invaluable lessons that setbacks impart allows us to lean into transformational experiences that offer opportunities to deepen our understanding and relationships with ourselves and the world. By embracing these lessons, we can learn to love more deeply, expand our consciousness, and step into a richer experience of life. Who doesn't want that?

There is no true defeat. When we adopt this perspective, we free ourselves from the weight of disappointment. Instead of succumbing to feelings of failure, we pivot very quickly and ask ourselves, "What can I learn from this?" This question opens doors to growth and exploration.

As I navigated my personal journey, I became increasingly aware of the interplay between the soul's work and heart energy versus the ego, which divides and separates. We've reflected on this in previous chapters, but understanding this relationship is crucial in using the law of relativity to its full potential.

Heart energy encompasses love, compassion, and understanding. When we connect with this energy, we can move beyond the ego's limitation, which often fuels judgment, fear, and separation. By embracing the heart's energy, we open ourselves to deeper connections with others.

What would it feel like if you accepted the lesson, if you pivoted, took accountability, and said, 'There is no right or wrong; There are only solutions'?" This is where the law of relativity comes in. It is solution-based. It is there to move you forward to what you desire.

Now, let's go back to the ego and heart energy because this plays a huge role in the law of relativity. The ego tends to cling to rigid beliefs and judgments, but it creates division within ourselves as well. In contrast, heart energy encourages us to embrace fluidity and compassion.

When we push beyond the ego's constraints, we can tap into a broader energy that fosters connection and unity. If we have not experienced this, it might feel daunting to have all that connection, all that unity, all that flow, but I can't tell you how beautiful this transition is.

To do this, we have to treat our experiences as teachers. That means there are no mistakes. We don't judge anything we've done. We just allow what has happened in our lives to teach us—and our experiences, whether joyful or painful, are our greatest teachers.

No one is going to have a more personal relationship with you than you. These experiences provide insights and lessons that enrich our understanding of life. Isn't it our responsibility to expand and understand where our capacity is? If not, we're limited by the ego energy, which keeps us stuck in a lack of movement and expansion.

Now, each moment offers this opportunity to learn about ourselves, our relationships, and the world around us. By embracing this perspective, we can cultivate gratitude for even the most challenging experiences.

I was born an intuitive, a knower, a seer. I didn't know that I could be that and that I could have my relationship with God and the safety that lived within me. It was either/or; it was pretty black and white. I didn't trust myself or my decisions.

Now that I'm an intuitive life coach, I know that God and the light that lives within me are my ultimate connection. By trusting my deep self, I removed the ego energy that once divided and separated me.

Before, I second-guessed everything and relied on everything external. Now, I trust everything internally. I draw on the deep knowing and knowledge that guides me. I forgive and acknowledge my past choices and self, and I recognize the lessons they taught me.

It is such a beautiful evolution. If you haven't experienced this, I want you to stop right now and ask yourself, "What can I release? What can I sacrifice and embrace?" You might desire a better relationship with someone, but your ego says, "I will never forgive them." What would it look like if you did? Because everything in our physical world is made real through its relationships to something else.

This is what the law of relativity means. We have a relationship with everything else. Nothing is ever sole and separate. We are all connected. What's negative for one person might not be for another, and your impact on another person could be exponential in their life if you allow it.

This law necessitates challenges and failures in exchange for a higher vibration and beauty in life. Are you willing to sacrifice for that beauty? My advice here is to fall greatly and fall often. There is no true defeat. Life's obstacles are opportunities to improve, understand more deeply, love more, and step into life's expansion. This soul work and heart energy push us beyond ego and into a more expansive energy.

Since you are reading this right now, it means you are yearning for something bigger and greater in your life. Do not dismiss that. I want you to sit and feel all the feelings. Nothing in this life is random. All events are connected and relative. I want you to appreciate the multifaceted nature of this existence.

So, lick your wounds, learn from your experiences, and grow. I love to set a timer and give myself five minutes to be angry, to be sad, to blow up, to do whatever I need to do. Then I move on.

You are not alone, and you have the power to change your path. This work requires you to examine your mistakes, understand your patterns, reflect on your choices, and analyze your beliefs.

Hiding from life prevents change, but the truth cannot be hidden.

So, identify and acknowledge your role in your circumstances. Do not spend a moment shaming yourself. Give yourself grace, forgiveness, and love with the understanding that the past version of you didn't know better.

I often like to revisit, giving grace, love, and forgiveness to different ages and stages of myself in my life. I let each version of me know how loved she is and how grateful I am. I wouldn't be here without her. If the expansion there tells me that the answer is always living within me, it's always living within you. You do not need special abilities or tools to find this out. You do not have to be born intuitive, but you have to learn to use the law of relativity to trust yourself in this expansion.

So, how can we use the law of relativity in our daily lives? Consider these practices and reflections, which can guide you on your one-on-one journey with yourself because it starts, my friends, with such a journey before you can connect with anyone else.

You must analyze how you are showing up. So, first, you do daily reflections. At the end of each day, take time to reflect on your experiences and ask yourself, "How did my perception shape my reactions today? What challenges did I encounter, and how could I view them as opportunities for growth? In what ways did I connect with my heart energy, and how did it influence my interactions? Or was I able to connect with my heart energy at all? Did I stay in defensive mode because it was safer?"

My friends, that's what the ego does. It divides and separates. It keeps you safe from fear—and fear represents false evidence that appears real. So, if you look at your interactions, are you looking at the fear, or are you actually looking at the truth? The fact is, the truth hasn't happened yet. The law of relativity says that if you change your heart energy, you change your connection to the world.

Now, I want you to write about a challenging experience and explore the different perspectives surrounding it. Consider how someone else might view the situation and what insights you can gain from that perspective. Incorporate mindfulness into your daily routine. That means taking a moment to pause and observe your thoughts and feelings without judgment. This practice can help you recognize the relativity of your emotions and the influence of your current context, the current stories that you're playing out.

Next, I'd like you to seek diverse perspectives. That means engaging in conversations with others who have different viewpoints. This exposure can not only broaden your understanding but can also give you an appreciation of relativity. By actively listening to others, you may uncover new insights that challenge your beliefs.

Now, if the ego is running the show, you're going to shut it down. So, you can see where your heart connection, expansiveness, and openness must be available to you to do this.

Next, I want to look at affirmations for accountability. You've used these in other universal laws, but here, you're using them differently. I want you to create affirmations that reinforce your commitment to accountability. For example, "I am responsible for my choices and the outcomes they create. I embrace challenges as opportunities for growth and learning." I want you to repeat these affirmations daily to cultivate a mindset of empowerment and resilience.

Practice gratitude because gratitude is the highest vibration we can use in the universe. Such a practice allows us to acknowledge the lessons that are learned from challenges. If you write down three things you're grateful for each day, focusing on how the obstacles have contributed to your growth, that's when the law of relativity really kicks in.

Next, I want you to engage with heart energy. That means incorporating practices that connect you with your heart energy. This can include meditation, acts of kindness, or simply taking moments to reflect on what brings you joy and fulfillment.

Allow this energy to guide your interactions and decisions. You must trust that these decisions and high vibrational energies are guided and that there are no mistakes. Using the law of relativity invites all of us to explore the interconnectedness of our experiences, emotions, and perceptions.

By embracing this law, we learn to navigate life's challenges with a renewed sense of purpose and understanding. Our past choices, while sometimes painful, serve as stepping stones toward greater wisdom and growth. The choices that got us here will not get us to the next level.

By recognizing that everything exists in relationship to something else, you can cultivate a more expansive and fulfilling existence that you have never experienced before. Ultimately, the law of relativity empowers you to take charge of your narrative. That means you are in control, and your greatest power is in how you show up, what you say, and what you receive.

Trust in your journey, embrace the lessons, and allow the beauty of the universal law of relativity to work for you, to let it guide you toward a deeper understanding of yourself and the world around you. Can you see how interconnected this universal law plays in the law of oneness, the law of vibration, the law of abundance, and the law of gender? They're all dancing together.

The law of relativity teaches us that nothing exists in isolation, that everything is interconnected and exists in relation to something else, and that principles can be applied to various aspects of life, including emotions, experiences, and perspectives.

Let's look at what that means. Our feelings and interpretations are often influenced by the context in which we find ourselves. For example, feelings of happiness may be amplified during a celebration, but they can feel different when experienced in solitude. Understanding this helps us appreciate the nuances of our emotional landscape and what we design. Think of your emotional landscape as a garden. If it's full of weeds and overgrown, what do you need to do to cultivate it? Where do you need to water? Where do you need to weed? Where do you need to fertilize? Where does it need more sunshine?

Your perspective is everything because the way we interpret events, situations, or even other people is deeply influenced by our past experiences, our religious beliefs, our personal beliefs, and our current state of mind. So, recognizing that relativity exists in every single interaction can not only foster empathy and understanding, but it allows us to see that others may perceive the same situation differently.

Isn't that what we want as a collective: to honor different perspectives and different and appreciate where others are coming from without judgment, anger, or resentment? We can hold space for all of it.

When faced with transitions, ask yourself, "How can I adapt with a new perspective to see the opportunities that are inherent in these changes?" This can help you navigate every bit of your life with grace and resilience.

Visualize your path. Imagine how different choices can lead to various outcomes. Your life is not set in stone, but it is set by the choices you are making. By contemplating the relativity of your decisions, you can make more informed choices that align with your desired path.

As we grow and expand in this life, we desire things differently. Can you imagine desiring what you wanted at 20, at 40? No, your desire is different; your information is different. Addressing the misconceptions about the law of relativity can enhance your application of its principles. There must be movement here.

Misconceptions about the law of relativity are common. Some may interpret relativity as a lack of clear truth. While perspectives differ, there are still universal truths that can guide us. Recognizing this balance can help us navigate complexities without losing sight of fundamental values.

Another misconception is that challenges are punishments. The universe never punishes. God does not punish. This misconception can lead to a victim mentality. Instead, view challenges as essential experiences that cultivate your growth.

The idea that relativity dismisses emotions is another false belief. Some might think that understanding relativity means minimizing emotional experiences. Just the opposite. Emotions are valid and significant, but recognizing relativity can help us contextualize and process them more effectively.

Yet another misconception is that everyone's experiences are similar. In reality, each person's background, beliefs, and emotions shape their perceptions. Everyone has a different filter. In fact, 90% of what everyone hears goes through their filter. They're only hearing 10% of what you're actually saying to them. Acknowledging this diversity fosters compassion and empathy, as you understand that everyone has their own story.

We can be compassionate for someone who is angry all the time. We may understand that there may be deep grief underneath and that they receive everything defensively and are angry because they do not have compassion for themselves yet or understand that the law of relativity can support them in their expansion.

Another misconception is that relativity leads to indecision. Instead, use it to inform your choices. Think of it as soul food that enriches your understanding of the situation so you can make not only an educated decision but a soulful one from a place of expansion. If we are making a decision from a limited space, a limited belief, the ego is in control and protecting us by dividing, separating, and judging.

The law of relativity invites you to explore the connections between you and your experiences, perceptions, and emotions. By recognizing that everything exists in relation to something else, you can cultivate a deeper understanding of your journey in this world and the lessons it offers because you are not alone. By embracing challenges, viewing them as opportunities for growth, taking accountability for your choices, and adopting a heart-centered approach, you can navigate life's complexities with grace and intention, integrate the law of relativity into your daily life and experiences, and let this be your greatest teacher. This will guide you to a more expansive and fulfilling existence than you have ever experienced.

The law of relativity invites you to self-discovery and growth, and this universal law is transformational and ongoing. It never stops. Trust in your capacity to learn from every experience. Trust that you know there's a lesson that can contribute to your evolution, that everything is applicable, that you can apply everything you learn, and that it can shift your relationship with everything and everyone. By embracing relativity, you allow it to empower you to create a life that aligns with your higher self.

Ask yourself, "What do I need today to get a different result? Am I willing to be accountable? Am I willing to stop playing the blame game? Am I willing to stop using the word 'but'? Can I apologize with just ownership?"

Next, I want you to write out three "I am" statements about what is in your life right now, your personal experience, and your challenges. Then, I want you to challenge the stories that have shaped your day-to-day patterns. Ground yourself in a new pattern.

The Mayo Clinic discovered that it takes 21 days to build a new habit. Can you commit to 21 days of activating and playing with this universal law of relativity? You're already working on it, but getting to know it and playing with it will allow you to manifest a story so expansive that you may want and seek complete accountability in everything you do.

There is nothing more freeing than using the law of relativity; it deepens your life and enriches it. Choose to lick your wounds, learn from life, and grow. You are not alone. The law of relativity tells you that you're connected to everything and that you have the power to change your paths.

The truth is that if you step into life expansion and decide to love more deeply, starting with yourself, the law of relativity will activate the universal law of vibration and the universal law of gender, and you will vibrate at a level that will support and expand your life with a velocity that I can't even articulate.

QUESTIONS FOR REFLECTION

What can you sacrifice and embrace?

_____

_____

_____

Are you willing to sacrifice for beauty in life?

_____

_____

_____

What challenges have you encountered recently, and how could you view them as opportunities for growth?

_____

_____

_____

In what ways did you connect with your heart energy, and how did it influence your interactions? Think of your emotional landscape as a garden—what do you need to do to cultivate it?

_____

_____

_____

When faced with transitions, how can you adapt to see the opportunities that are inherent in the changes?

_____

_____

_____

Are you willing to be accountable and stop playing the blame game?

_____

_____

_____

CHAPTER 11
BODY BALANCE
UNIVERSAL LAW OF MASCULINE AND FEMININE

"If you drop duality, you become whole—and in that wholeness is real holiness."
~ Osho

My journey with the law of gender is an interesting one. It has profoundly shaped my understanding of balance in my life, particularly through my personal experiences with physical injuries and healing.

I found myself breaking my left toe multiple times over the last couple of years. Each time it happened, I felt frustrated and confused. The left side of my body seemed to be signaling something.

In understanding the law of gender, it's essential to recognize how our bodies reflect our internal states. The left side of our body is associated with feminine energy, receptivity, nurturing, and intuition, while the right side embodies masculine energy, assertiveness, action, and logic. This division is not just metaphorical. It is a physical representation of how we engage with the world.

THE LIE: *The left and right sides of our bodies are just physical. Things are random, and we do not have yin and yang in the body.*

THE TRUTH: *The left side of the body is feminine for receiving, and the right side is masculine, where we show up for output action. They represent our dual nature. We are not one or the other. We must integrate and use the powers of receiving and giving, the yin and yang, and identify where we are out of balance. Our job is to understand what we are under- and over-delivering.*

As I explored the connections between my physical injuries and the law of gender, I realized that my struggles with receiving were manifesting physically. It is so powerful to understand that we are not separate from our physical bodies. Louise Hay wrote a wonderful book about this, *How to Heal Your Life*, which I highly recommend you read.

As I reflected on my energy and injuries, I realized that my left side, my receiving side, was calling for my attention. I needed to nurture my feminine energies and embrace the act of receiving.

As an overachiever and type-A personality, I have always struggled with this. To find the balance, I began to practice self-care, allowing myself to rest and receive help from others. I cultivated an environment of love and support.

At the same time, I realized that I had often overemphasized doing and achieving at the expense of being receptive. Understanding this dynamic helped me integrate both energies more harmoniously, and I soon noticed a significant shift in my life.

I no longer experienced injuries only on my left side. Instead, I found myself more grounded and in tune with my body's needs. This highlighted several key points about the interplay of masculine and feminine energies, and I really started paying attention to them.

Balance is so essential. The law of gender teaches us that both masculine and feminine energies are necessary for a fulfilling life. When we lean too heavily into one energy, we risk creating imbalances that can manifest as physical ailments or emotional distress.

Ask yourself, "Is one side of my body more injured than the other? Do I get headaches on one side and not the other?" Pay attention to where you are incurring injuries.

By nurturing both sides, we create a harmonious flow that supports our overall well-being. The body knows the way. In my case, repetitive injuries were a clear signal that I needed to reevaluate how I was engaging with the world. Paying attention to physical clues can not only reveal areas where we may be out of balance but also where we need to shift our approach.

I learned that allowing support and love into my life did not signify weakness. Rather, it was a powerful act of self-love and acknowledgment of my worthiness. This shift not only improved my physical health but also deepened my connection with those around me.

The manifestation of masculine and feminine energies in our actions is vital. When I was overly focused on achievement, I found myself becoming more aggressive and competitive. I also compared myself to others. Ego energy supports this masculine energy. By allowing my feminine side to flourish, I became more empathetic and nurturing, creating a space where both energies could coexist.

Recognizing the signs of imbalance in our lives is crucial to understanding the law of gender. Here are some indicators to look for.

We're going to start with physical symptoms. Notice if you frequently experience injuries or tension in one side of your body. Injuries on the left side can indicate a struggle with receiving, while those on the right might point to overextending and action without balance.

Your emotional patterns may reflect how you handle stress and challenges. Do you find yourself pushing through without asking for help? Are you overly emotional and lacking boundaries? These patterns may signal an imbalance between your masculine and feminine energies.

Examine your relationships. Are you giving more than you are receiving? Are you an over-giver, or are you a taker? Are you taking too much without considering the needs of others? Understanding these dynamics can help you adjust your approach.

Embrace receptivity. Create opportunities to receive love and support. This may involve asking for help, and it may be uncomfortable for those of you who are doers and givers. Accept compliments graciously or simply allow yourself to relax and recharge, and maybe even accept gifts.

Love languages come into play with the law of gender, so if you haven't yet done the *Love Language Quiz*, I encourage you to google it and do that.

Nurturing your feminine energies can be as simple as engaging in creative pursuits like painting, cooking, or dancing. Engage in an activity that allows you to connect with your intuition and express yourself freely. My creative expression comes in the form of doodling—there is a doodle page in every workbook I create.

Next, I want you to establish clear boundaries in your relationships. This will allow you to protect your energy and ensure that your giving and receiving are balanced. Otherwise, we will soon be depleted, and burnout will exist. Of the five stages of stress, burnout is the last one. Setting boundaries will keep you in the flow and nurture of your life.

The next one is mindfulness and reflection. Take time to meditate and reflect on your relationships with both of these energies. Ask yourself, "Where do I feel balanced? Where do I need to nourish one side or the other? Am I in balance? Am I out of balance? Do I understand the law of gender? How is it playing out in my life? Where can I use the law of gender more?"

Next, I'm going to go into physical movement here because exercise will help you connect with both of these energies.

Yoga, for example, can help balance and strengthen both sides of the body, promoting harmony between the masculine and the feminine. This is why I love yoga. It allows you to hold space, connect the body's energies, and understand the positive and negative manifestations of the law of gender.

Knowing that the law of gender can show up in both positive and negative ways in your life is so important to acknowledge. First, I want to look at positive manifestations. This is a balanced approach to life that allows creativity, fulfillment, and meaningful connections.

When both energies are nurtured, you can engage in healthy relationships, make empowered decisions, and manifest your desires effectively. What does your life look like? Are you in healthy relationships? Does your life feel balanced? Are you overworking? Do you have healthy boundaries?

Next, I want to look at a negative manifestation. This is an imbalance that can lead to frustration, burnout, and dissatisfaction.

Previously, we discussed the five levels of stress, with burnout being the last one. We can often find ourselves there if we do not have a balance with the law of gender. Over-identifying with the masculine may result in aggression and competition, while leaning too heavily into the feminine can lead to emotional overwhelm and a lack of direction.

Recognize that nurturing both the masculine and the feminine energies is essential not only for overall well-being but also to experience a more poignant sense of balance, receptivity, and self-love. We must be in harmony with this law.

As you navigate your relationship with these energies, I want you to remember that both exist within you already, and which one you nurture will be vital for your growth and manifestation. By embracing the lessons from my personal story and paying attention to my injuries, I cultivated a deeper understanding of the law of gender, how it could positively influence my life, and what changes I needed to make. When I made them, my life grew exponentially, not only in terms of love and joy but also money.

I want you to think of the law of gender as balance within your body —the yin and the yang. Ask yourself, "Where may I be out of balance?" Trust that nurturing both sides of yourself is absolutely doable and embrace the transformative power that arises from this integration. When your body is in balance, you are unstoppable.

Your journey towards balance is not only a personal endeavor but a universal one as well. Celebrating the beautiful dance of masculine and feminine energies that exists within all of us is what we strive for. Whether we acknowledge it or not, it is what the subconscious constantly yearns for.

The law of gender states that everything, including energy, has a masculine and feminine aspect. Not only do these energies play a critical role in how we manifest our desires, but they're how we navigate our world.

Stop right now and look at how you are navigating your world. Are these two energies in balance? Have you acknowledged the feminine and the masculine side, or is this the first time that the idea has been introduced to you?

By knowing this, you can create a harmonious environment for growth, creativity, and fulfillment that you've not yet tapped into. Our goal here is to be expansive and allow these universal laws to dance and support our lives.

Once again, masculine energy is associated with action, logic, structure, and assertiveness, and it embodies qualities such as leadership, strength, and decisiveness. Masculine energy is the driving force that propels us toward our goals.

Using the masculine energy is powerful, but it is the feminine energy, linked to intuition, receptivity, nurturing, and creativity, that radiates love and light and holds a space for ideas and inspirations to flourish. Can you see where the soul food is here that feeds the masculine energy? The feminine energy is essential for allowing creativity to unfold and for receiving the gifts that life has to offer.

When one of these energies is shut down, we are living at 50%. We need 100% to move. Continuous action without the ability to receive can lead to burnout, while excessive receptivity without action can result in stagnation.

Here's how you can harness both of these energies effectively. This is where you're really going to want to lean in and take notes.

Assess your balance and consider where you are in your life right now. Do you constantly find yourself achieving and pushing forward, or are you often waiting for things to come to you? Are you overly competitive and aggressive, or do you lack boundaries and find it hard to take action? How do you show up in your relationships? Are you nurturing, or are you too assertive?

Common signs of a lack of feminine energy are difficulty trusting your instincts, overthinking, and feeling stuck in a cycle of doing without receiving.

Excessive masculine energy will show up as aggressiveness, competitiveness, and a tendency to dominate situations or people. Another symptom is talking over people without giving them the opportunity to respond.

The concept of yin and yang beautifully encapsulates the essence of the law of gender. Yin represents the feminine energy, receptive, nurturing, and intuitive, while yang embodies the masculine energy, assertiveness, action-oriented, and logical. Together, they create a complete whole.

The feminine energy is like a seed. It requires nurturing and space to grow. This energy must be received in honor, allowing it to flourish.

The masculine energy acts as pollen. It provides the necessary action and movement to facilitate growth. It holds space for the feminine to express and manifest its creation.

For creative activation, we must balance these energies. As Matthew 7:7 says, *"Ask, and it shall be given to you."* This principle emphasizes the importance of receptivity in the creative process. If we ask, it shall be given to us.

Next, let's look at the chakra system, which serves as a profound tool for understanding the balance of the masculine and the feminine energies. Each chakra resonates with specific energies and can influence our overall well-being.

We'll start with the first chakra, the root chakra. That is the masculine chakra, and it's located at the base of the spine. This chakra is associated with stability, security, and grounding. It represents our connection to the physical world and is often linked to the masculine qualities of strength and determination.

The second chakra is the sacral chakra, which is feminine. Found in the lower abdomen, this chakra governs creativity, sexuality, and emotions. It embodies feminine energy, emphasizing fluidity and nurturing.

The third is the solar plexus chakra, which is masculine. Located in the upper abdomen, this chakra is linked to personal power, competence, and self-esteem. It represents the assertive aspects of masculine energy.

Number four is the heart chakra, which has feminine energy. Situated in the center of the chest, this chakra embodies love, compassion, and connection. It is a bridge between masculine and feminine energies and facilitates balance.

Number five is the throat chakra, which is masculine. It's located at the throat. This chakra governs communication and self-expression. It reflects the assertiveness and clarity of the masculine energy.

Six is the third-eye chakra. We're back to the feminine. This chakra is positioned in the center of the forehead and is associated with intuition, insight, and inner wisdom. It embodies the receptive and intuitive qualities of feminine energy.

Now, number seven is the crown chakra, which is also feminine. Found at the top of the head, this chakra connects us to the higher consciousness and our spiritual awareness. It represents the nurturing and expansive qualities of feminine energy.

To achieve a balance between masculine and feminine energies, I want you to consider incorporating the following tools and practices into your daily routine.

First, let's get grounded in some crystals. I really love rose quartz because it embodies feminine energy and promotes love, compassion, and emotional healing. Use it to embrace your feminine qualities and nurture self-love.

The green turtle crystal line is excellent for heart connection, fostering love and compassion for yourself and others. I'm only going to give you those two because I really want you to stay in the heart energy connected to all the energies.

Next, we're going to look at meditation and reflection. Dedicate time each day to meditate on your energies. Visualize the balance of the masculine and the feminine within you. Allow both energies to flow harmoniously. Visualize them as dancing together.

Another tool is to pay attention to your body. Are your injuries on one side of your body more than the other? If so, this could indicate an imbalance. Frequent injuries on the left side may suggest a lack of feminine energy, while injuries on the right side could indicate an excess of masculine energy.

Creative expression is also a powerful tool. Engage in activities that nurture your feminine energy, such as cooking, painting, and playing music. For me, it was doodling. Allow yourself to explore creativity so your intuition can expand. Trust in a deeper understanding of yourself.

I want you to ground in activities using your first chakra. Incorporate grounding practices to strengthen your masculine energy. This may include physical exercise, spending time in nature, or engaging in assertive activities that require focus and determination. Assess your relationships and identify where you need to establish healthier boundaries. Are you giving too much, or are you not receiving enough? Use this insight to foster balance.

To further explore your relationship with the masculine and feminine energies, consider following reflective practices. Write about your experiences and feelings related to both energies. Reflect on moments when you feel balanced or imbalanced and what contributed to those feelings.

Do an energy assessment. Reflect on which energy you lean into more. Are you more action-oriented or receptive? Access areas of your life where you need more balance.

Regularly check in with your emotions. Are you feeling overly emotional or disconnected? Use these cues to inform your journey toward balance.

It's important to know the pros and cons associated with this law. Regarding pros, it promotes self-awareness and an understanding of internal dynamics. It encourages balance in relationships and personal life. It facilitates creative expression and manifestation. It aids in emotional healing and personal growth.

One of the cons is that misunderstanding the balance can lead to frustration or confusion. Another is that over-identifying with one energy may result in burnout or stagnation. Societal expectations may pressure people to conform to traditional gender roles. Know that you can put all of these things back in balance.

A common misconception is that masculine and feminine energies strictly align with gender. In reality, everyone possesses both energies regardless of gender identity.

People also often mistakenly believe that feminine energy is weak. This is a misconception of epic proportions. In truth, feminine energy embodies strength, nurturing, intuition, and expansion that can take your life to unbelievable heights.

The next misconception is that masculine energy is the only path to success. Do, do, do. Go, go, go. Slay, slay, slay. Some believe that success requires an exclusively masculine approach. However, balance between both these energies is essential for holistic achievement. If you want to create a sustainable life, you will need to incorporate both.

Another misconception is that emotional expression equals weakness. This misconception often stifles the feminine aspect. In reality, expressing emotion is the most powerful and essential part of the human experience. Allow yourself to feel. There is no spiritual bypassing, and the only way through is through. No dodging emotions here. If you want what you want, you must learn to feel.

THE TRUTH WITHIN THE LIE

The next misconception is that you must choose one energy over the other. Many feel they may operate primarily from either masculine or feminine energy. The truth is that embracing both energies leads to a balanced, fulfilling life that gives you what you desire.

As you embark on this journey, remember that both energies are essential for manifestation, creativity, and growth. By embracing and nurturing the qualities of the feminine energy while honoring the assertiveness of the masculine, your growth will be exponential. However, it's never a one-and-done.

If your life is out of balance, I invite you to integrate these insights and practices into your daily life. You will not only enhance your understanding of the law of gender but also pave the way for a balanced life that may not exist in your life now.

If you could implement one thing right now, what would it be? I want you to trust in the process and honor the energies that flow within you, for they hold the keys to your growth and transformation.

Ask, and you shall receive. This creativity must be activated to release the energies for transformation. The lie is that it's not available to you, that you must have one or the other.

The truth is that we were all born with masculine and feminine energies, and you can use the feminine to balance the masculine and vice versa. A block in one of the energies indicates the need for balance.

Pay attention to where you're holding energies. We are made up of energy. The chakras are just different energies in your body. Get to know where you're holding energy, where you're blocked, and perhaps where you have illnesses or injuries.

I highly recommend reading Louise Hay's book, *Heal Your Body*. It will help you connect what's going on in your body physically to what is going on energetically, and it will give you a mantra to shift that energy.

Reflect on the energies and lean into the yin and the yang. There's no right or wrong here. Dance with these energies and get to know your physical and spiritual-ness by using the law of gender.

QUESTIONS FOR REFLECTION

Are you giving more than you are receiving?

_____

_____

_____

Are you taking too much without considering the needs of others?

_____

_____

_____

Where do you feel balanced?

_____

_____

_____

THE TRUTH WITHIN THE LIE

Where do you need to nourish one side or the other?

_____

_____

_____

Do you have healthy boundaries?

_____

_____

_____

Have you acknowledged your feminine and masculine sides, or is this the first time that the idea has been introduced to you?

_____

_____

_____

Do you constantly find yourself achieving and pushing forward, or are you often waiting for things to come to you?

_____

_____

_____

Are you overly competitive and aggressive, or do you lack boundaries and find it hard to take action?

_____

_____

_____

CHAPTER 12
ARE YOU READY?
THE LAW OF SUCCESS

*"The starting point of all achievement is desire.
Keep this constantly in mind. Weak desire brings weak results,
just as a small fire makes a small amount of heat."*
~ Napoleon Hill

I can't identify the law of success without thinking of the quote, "He can who thinks he can." This powerful quote attributed to Virgil, the ancient Roman poet, resonates deeply with me as it implies that everyone is intended to succeed. Yes, you're intended to succeed.

In the eyes of the divine, there is no hierarchy. We are all born equal, imbued with the potential to achieve greatness. It is God's will that people not only use but also enjoy the abundant resources of the universe.

The love of the divine denies us nothing. Thus, we are inherently rich in potential. The law of success has no limitations.

It is an inexhaustible force that resides within each of us, waiting to be tapped into. The journey to success is not only about external achievements but also about internal growth and self-discovery. As we dive in and explore the law of success, we must recognize that while the universe is abundant, our beliefs and stories can limit us.

So, let's define the law of success. Really, it's the principle that success is available to everyone willing to pursue it with intention, effort, and persistence. It encompasses the idea that success is not merely a destination but a journey defined by our choices, actions, and mindsets. As you can see, that is a theme with every universal law, our choices, our actions, and our mindsets. The law of success really embraces and fosters an abundant mindset, allowing us to see opportunities rather than limitations.

Understanding that success is achievable empowers us to take charge of our lives and pursue every aspiration that we can dream of. It also encourages us to pursue continuous growth, learning, and self-improvement.

Now, I'm going to dive in right away with the pros and cons of the law of success because I believe people get hung up here a lot.

Society emphasizes success; it can create undue pressure and anxiety and lead us to feel inadequate and overwhelmed. How many of you have felt overwhelmed by external expectations of what success looks like in your life? We may fall into the trap of comparing our success to others, undermining our self-worth on our unique journeys.

I often refer to the need to put blinders on, just like a horse does in a horse race, where you cannot see the other horses and stay in your lane. This is your personal relationship to success. Comparing it to the relationship of others is the thief of not only your success but of joy, which feeds success. Ultimately, it undermines your self-worth and derails your process.

Misunderstanding about what success truly entails can lead us to chase hollow achievements and neglect our personal fulfillment. Once again, I want to look at the stories that we create and our limitations around success.

Often, the stories we tell ourselves about success can be the barrier that hinders our progress. These narratives are often shaped by societal expectations, our past experiences, and personal self-doubt, and they can lead to limiting beliefs that restrict our potential. What would it look like if you had no stories about what you could do and what your relationship to success is?

On my journey, I initially defined success through my external achievements. Working for a business lobbyist group, I was celebrated for setting still unbroken records. This is where it gets tricky. Due to this identity being superficial.

It was built on a foundation of societal approval rather than authentic self-worth. This is where I set myself up for self-sabotage. I did not feel worthy of that achievement, so when I achieved it, I did not know how to maintain it because my self-worth was at a minimum. What I was achieving was at a premium, and the two didn't align. I could not hold space for both.

This is common when we are not in alignment with the universal law of success. When I engaged in the deep, personal work of redefining success on my terms, I discovered that true success involves not only transparency and deep self-love but also the courage to confront my insecurities, to share what I believed was true about myself and go back and love that version of myself. This inner work revealed that the real essence of success lies in personal achievements. It has nothing to do with the external world.

THE LIE: *I wasn't worthy of success, and I didn't know enough. And without a law degree, who was I?*

THE TRUTH: *The truth is, we will never rise and achieve what is possible. We will always fall back to where we believe our worthiness is. Remember, your self-worth is determined by you. It is never attached to letting people tell us who we are.*

I manifested everything in my life, whether it be a lesson or an achievement. I called it all in to evolve. My successes were real no matter how much I wanted to discredit myself or self-sabotage. The truth is that I deserved all this success. I put in the work, and I was smart enough and talented enough. The ability to share abundance with others ultimately benefited a larger community, this connectedness that we'll later talk about in the universal law of oneness.

So, I want you to know that there are infinite resources, and there is so much magic in the power of imagination. The universe is filled with infinite resources that are available to you right now if you're willing to seek them. Success is not confined to a singular path, but it embraces a multitude of possibilities. The key lies in harnessing the power of imagination and believing in the potential within.

Here are the questions I want you to consider right now. What is it you truly desire? What do you want to achieve? Do you expect to succeed? What is your relationship to success? Has your life up until this point been disappointing? Are you willing to illuminate a new path and let that guide you? The answer to these questions can guide your current actions.

I say again: the only limitations on success are self-imposed. The stories you create can dictate your potential, but you have the power to rewrite them. At this very moment, you have the power to change your relationship to success.

When discussing the true nature of success, it is essential to understand that it means different things to different people. While many associate success with wealth or status, true success transcends material possessions. Success starts in the soul; it starts in the heart energy.

Genuine success lies in the results obtained, the impacts made, and the ability to share the success with others, to be able to connect. It reflects a harmonious balance of personal fulfillment and collective benefits.

People will often say, "I've succeeded, but this isn't the way I thought it would feel." Despite their perceived success, they feel empty and hollow. That is exactly what I'm talking about. Success on a deeper, soulful level must be connected to others.

True success is about growth, the favorable termination of endeavors, and the constructive use of life's elements to build ourselves up. It involves nurturing self-esteem, self-worth, and the recognition that we are entitled to pursue our dreams at any age. The great interference with success often comes from within. We can hinder our progress through self-doubt, fear, and limited beliefs.

We must confront these internal barriers and develop strategies to overcome them. Here are some tools for overcoming this self-interference.

Number one is self-reflection. Regularly assess your beliefs about success. Are they serving you? Are they holding you back?

The second one is practicing mindfulness. Become aware of negative thought patterns and replace them with positive affirmations. Flip the narrative.

Number three, especially if life isn't giving you what you want, is goal setting. Establish clear, achievable goals that align with your personal definition of success. Break them down into actionable steps. One of my clients is a very successful doctor. He never wanted to be a doctor. His father was a doctor, so he felt obligated to become one when what he wanted to do was be an environmentalist. He wanted to work in the woods. Now, after working with me, he's no longer a doctor. I'm happy to say that he is living his life according to his true desire. He used his power of imagination to remove himself from the expectations that weren't aligned with his desires and his idea of success.

The lesson here is that what you can envision in your mind, you can create in the material world. By fostering a clear vision of what success looks like and feels like, you empower yourself to take actionable steps toward achieving it. Once you start thinking about it, your life changes to match your thoughts. You will then start to lean in and take small actions that maybe you're not even aware of yet.

Remember that success is not only a personal journey, but it's defined by your core values, deep desires, and aspirations. The stories you tell yourself have so much power. They shape your reality. Therefore, they choose the narratives that empower and uplift you.

True success is not measured solely by wealth or status but by the positive impact you have on your world and the fulfillment you find in the endeavors you choose. As I've said before, your highest power is the right to choose. Embrace this infinite potential and confront your limitations.

Confront the terror barrier and recognize and take action toward your dreams. You deserve success—it is your birthright—and the universe is abundant with opportunities that are just waiting for you to seize them.

My goal in highlighting the universal law of success is to provide you with the depth, clarity, and personal insight to recreate a new relationship with it and allow you to take actionable steps toward it. Now let's go a little bit deeper into expanding the law.

Let's look at having a growth mindset versus a fixed mindset. A growth mindset, the belief that abilities and intelligence can be developed through dedication and hard work, contrasts with a fixed mindset, which assumes that our capabilities are static.

Embracing a growth mindset encourages resilience in the face of challenges. It allows you to view failures as opportunities for learning rather than insurmountable obstacles. You can adopt a growth mindset by interrupting and reframing negative thoughts. For instance, instead of thinking, *"I can't do this,"* you might say, *"I can't do this yet, but I will learn."*

Passion plays a huge role in success. It is the pathway. When we engage in activities that we love, we are more likely to invest time, energy, and money in them, leading to a greater sense of fulfillment and achievement. We must divorce from the outcome and stay married to the process of success, not the outcome.

What excites you at this moment? I want you to explore trying a new activity, reflect on a childhood interest, or identify moments when you felt most alive. Go back and see what and how they lit you up and how connected you were to them. Then ask yourself. "Where along the way did I disconnect from that passion and that part of my story?"

When passion aligns with purpose, success becomes more obtainable. Understand that your unique talents and interests can guide you to your true calling. There is only one you, and the importance of perseverance is your personal story.

We're going to face adversity and resistance, but success is rarely a straight path. It often involves setbacks and challenges. Resilience is the ability to bounce back from difficulties, and it's crucial for long-term success. Understand that these roadblocks are guiding us, and the closer we come to a larger, bigger life, the more resistance we will find. That is a sign that we're on the right track.

Building resilience is a huge foundation for success, as are developing a strong support network and practicing self-care, particularly during adversity. Self-care is your number-one go-to. It's also important to maintain a positive outlook, even through tough times.

Here's a self-assessment exercise that you can do right now. Ask yourself, "What does success look like to me? How do I want to feel when I achieve my goals? What values are most important to me in my journey toward success?"

There is no right or wrong here. The ego will come in and judge, divide, and separate. It will say, "That's right, and this is wrong," and separate you from your success. Allow every decision you make to guide you. Even if an action doesn't take you where you want to go, it's still valuable because it tells you that a particular direction is the wrong one.

It's also important to understand that success is often facilitated by the relationships we build. We often hear people say, "If it weren't for that person or connection, I wouldn't have had that opportunity." People also say, "A rising tide lifts all boats." When someone in our support network succeeds, the tide rises for all of us. In other words, when people come together to support one another, they amplify their chances of success.

One tool for achieving success is setting "SMART" goals. These goals are specific, measurable, achievable, relevant, and time-bound. This framework will help you create clear, actionable goals.

The idea is to transform vague aspirations into SMART goals. For instance, instead of saying, "I want to be healthy," you can say, "I will exercise for 30 minutes a day, three times a week, for the next three months." That is an actionable, SMART goal.

Now let's talk about ways to overcome fear. Fear is a barrier that allows us to loop back into old stories. It paralyzes us, preventing us from taking risks or pursuing anything further. It pits the comfort zone versus the home zone.

Understanding that failure is a natural part of the path toward success can help mitigate fear. Not only do we want to reframe fear, but we want to become friends with it. We want to say, "Oh, I understand why you're here. You're here because you're challenging me. You're here to fuel me."

Think of failure as a stepping stone rather than an endpoint. Successful clients of mine who have faced failures use them as learned experiences. I often say we eat failures for breakfast. They are our Wheaties. We look at what we've done, we remember, and we allow the experience to guide us. We do not take anything personally. We are grateful for the fear that shows up because we take action through it anyway.

Fear is always present. With every stage I step on, I'm always fearful, but I allow that fear. I flip the coin, and on the other side is excitement, and I allow that energy. With every step I take on that stage, I recognize that I am there for a reason. Even when fear is present, even when it could shut me down, it illuminates, and I allow it to be my soul food.

I also want to emphasize that gratitude equals success. My clients do gratitude practices every day, writing down three things they're grateful for. Rather than focusing on what they lack, they create a positive mindset that not only attracts more abundance but makes success imminent. A focus on positivity not only shifts your perspective, fostering a sense of fulfillment, but it also raises your vibration to attract more success, calling in people who are like-minded and energetically connected.

This is where we balance our ambition and well-being with our success. I look at success as being holistic because it encompasses not just professional achievements but personal well-being. It's essential to strike a balance between ambition and self-care.

It can't be all self-care, and it can't be all ambition. Instead, we blend them, we hold space for them, we dance with them, and we keep that pendulum in balance. We constantly ask ourselves, "Am I grateful for what I've learned? Am I grateful for this moment? Am I grateful for the success I've achieved so far?"

Nurturing your physical, emotional, and mental well-being, which may include exercise, mindfulness, creative pursuits, or spending quality time with loved ones, feeds your success. There is nothing that creates success more than being connected. Isolating yourself with a slay-the-day, overdriven nature and the need to compete only makes the struggle for success harder.

I want you to ask yourself lovingly and with kindness: "Where am I at with my relationships with these?" It's never too late to re-establish a relationship with yourself. Prioritize your self-care practices, nourish your physical body, and stay grateful and connected to yourself. If you don't, burnout is imminent.

I want to highlight the importance of recognizing the signs of burnout, and I want you to take proactive steps to recharge now. If you feel uninspired, exhausted, like life has spun out of control, or that you're paying a huge price for your success, I want you to know that success should not come at the expense of health and happiness. Taking charge of your success is your responsibility.

In this deep dive into the law of success, I want to remind you that you not only possess the power of success, but you have the power to shape your destiny and redefine success because it is not a destination. It is a continuous path of growth, joy, learning, and contribution. By embracing this abundant mindset, clarifying your personal definitions of success, and taking intentional action, you can unlock your unbelievable, infinite potential.

Your story is still being written, and you have the power to redefine what it means to succeed. You can flip your story right now, change directions, and have unbelievable success if you're willing to take the risk and challenge what success looks and feels like. Is the success story you're living even your story?

If you find yourself facing challenges on your road to success, I want you to embrace them. In fact, I want you to seek out difficulties. Actively look for challenges that push you out of your comfort zone.

This could involve taking on new projects at work, trying new activities, and learning new skills. The terror barrier is there for one reason: to keep you in your comfort zone. Your subconscious is saying, "I'm afraid of this because it's new."

Challenge yourself to step past the newness. Recognize that success lies on the other side of doing something new. View these challenges as opportunities for exponential growth rather than obstacles to avoid. Never take failure personally. Encourage feedback and constructive criticism from peers, mentors, and supervisors. Use this feedback as a valuable tool to improve rather than a personal attack on you.

Take time to reflect on feedback and identify the areas in which you can grow. Consider how you can apply any of this feedback to any future endeavor that perhaps you've been cultivating or dreaming about.

Celebrate the efforts, not just the results. As I said before, it's not about the destination. It's about the path that gets us there.

I want you to acknowledge your hard work up to this point. I want you to recognize and celebrate the efforts that you've put into tasks, regardless of the outcome. Divorce yourself from the outcome; stay married to the process. For example, aim to practice a skill for a certain number of hours rather than solely focusing on achieving a specific outcome.

While writing this book. I'm not looking at what the outcome is going to be. Instead, I'm looking at how the chapters are unfolding. Am I connected to my story? Am I connected to the truth? Am I offering value and a service to the reader?

This is about leveraging the power of "yet." I want you to use positive language when facing difficulties. Incorporate the word "yet." This is an incredible, powerful move. Instead of saying, "I cannot do this," say, "I cannot do this yet." This simple shift—and boy, you know I like to keep it simple—emphasizes the potential for growth.

I also encourage you to encourage others. Not only will you encourage them, but I can guarantee you that it will reflect similar perspectives back to you, potentially illuminating solutions to your own challenges. We are all connected in oneness and practicing self-compassion.

I can't emphasize this next point enough: be kind to yourself. Treat yourself with the same compassion that you would extend to a friend or a loved one experiencing setbacks. Acknowledge that everyone faces difficulties and learning a path. Avoid self-criticism, replacing negative self-talk with positive affirmations.

Focus on what you can do and learn from a mistake instead of dwelling on perceived failures or what could happen. Be curious about it. I want you to ignite a passion for learning and growing because that is what success is. It's about exploring something. It's about cultivating curiosity. It's about asking deeper, more insightful questions about where you are in your life. When you do that, you call in other people on that same frequency.

That builds a supportive network. Connect with people who embody a growth mindset. Their attitudes and behaviors can inspire you to adopt a similar belief and practice.

That's what we're doing. We're practicing. There is no perfection.

Engage in growth-oriented discussions. Find a group. Join Toastmasters and participate in conversations where people are learning, improving, and overcoming challenges. There is nothing you cannot overcome. This can reinforce your commitment to a growth mindset.

And reflect on your experiences. I love keeping a journal, not only to record daily experiences and challenges but also successes. It is so important to focus on your small successes. When you do, every day that you wake up, open your eyes, and breathe is a success. Writing down your thoughts can help you not only process your feelings but also recognize patterns in your life, growth, and success.

The subconscious allows us to stay numb. We have a minimum of 65,000 thoughts a day. Are they successful thoughts? Do they feed a successful mindset, or are they stories that keep us on the other side of the terror barrier, stuck in a life that does not allow us to step into the life that we might be dreaming about, but don't think is possible?

Well, I'm here to let you know it is possible, and I want to start by helping you set realistic expectations. I want you to understand the learning curve. Recognize that mastery takes time and effort. Set realistic expectations about the pace of your progress and be patient with yourself.

Focus on incremental improvements. Celebrate small milestones along the way. That means listening, writing them down, and telling yourself who you are. Don't let yourself be defined by who someone else is. Do not seek external validation. Instead, I want you to write down and tell me who you are.

Write down three things right now that can contribute to your growth. So stay committed to this as a lifelong learning process. When we lean in, expand, and call in the universal law of success, it means that we are pursuing continuous education.

That can look different for everyone, but I want to encourage you to look up and see what you've always wanted to do. Look up courses. Look up workshops. Read a book that takes you out of your comfort zone and into a growth mindset. Be receptive to new perspectives and ideas, even if they challenge your existing beliefs.

This openness fosters adaptability and growth beyond your self-assigned capacity. This is why I say, "Stay married to the process; divorce the outcome." If you allow this growth mindset, the outcome is larger than anything you could put in its place. So, stay very married to the process because, when you do, the growth is exponential.

And remember that growth is a journey. Every step you take contributes to the development of something new; allow yourself to let that expand. I have a client in her seventies who was a wife and a mother. When I met with her, she said, "I don't know what I want. I don't know what I want." But one day, she opened up and said, "You know, I went to art school many years ago, and I still play in that field." Now, a year later, she is an extraordinarily successful artist. She took ownership of her dream, and her imposter syndrome is gone.

Imposter syndrome is something that will block the law of success. She did not consider herself an artist because she identified as something else. But when she started to believe that she was worthy enough to recreate her life—and it's never too late—she became a successful artist and is now selling her work. I love this story because her relationship with success has changed exponentially, and I celebrate it daily.

So, achieving success is about reframing your setbacks, reframing your identity, and how you see yourself. If you want the law of success to work for you, you must look inward for the true measure of what that means, not outward. Don't judge yourself. Only look at what and how you can expand and what you can learn from yourself.

This law asks you to assess your current life situation and personal relationship with success. Success is not about what the world wants of you or how you show up. It is about these pivotal moments, just you, your integrity, and how you want to define your life.

When we're on our deathbeds, we don't talk about what we were in this life but how we felt successful. Were we successful in love? Were we successful as a mom? Were we successful in relationships? Were we willing to risk changing our lives? If you do not believe you are worthy of success, you will likely sabotage yourself.

I did many, many times until I learned to love myself, went back to all the versions of myself that I had shamed, and told them how grateful I was that they went through what they did. I grieved with them to become one with the law of success. Every version of myself got me here. I cannot shame my path and celebrate my success now. Every version led to the success that I obtained and now celebrate.

Success often begins in childhood. It's rooted in the values and beliefs that our families instill. For many, the narrative around success was shaped by parental expectations, cultural norms, and family achievements. This can be not only generational, as I've talked about before, but also time-stamped.

In different eras, we are expected to do different things. Would I have thought that people could make millions of dollars being influencers on social media platforms 20 years ago? No, as 20 years ago, many of us didn't even have cell phones.

So, we have to stay open to the changing times and our relationship to success. Consider someone who grew up in a family that prioritized education. Now, I work with someone whose family focuses on education. Everything is about education. She has multiple degrees. Everyone in her family has a master's degree.

She wants to be a life coach, but she doesn't believe her family will value her choice. You can complete programs, you can be certified, and you can be a master life coach, but there isn't a doctorate in life coaching. So, her family does not value this profession, thinking of it more as a trade or service.

As you can see, the success of siblings or parents who excelled academically can pressure us to achieve similar heights. We may internalize the belief that success equates with academic excellence, leading to anxiety and the fear of failure. It took this client everything to hire me, lean in, and hold space and the terror of what she loves. And I'm going to tell you, she's an extraordinary coach with a multitude of master's degrees. It is her psyche and her relationship to success, education, her parents, and expectations that hold her back.

In contrast, for someone from a family that values artistic expression, success might be an ability to create and innovate. This perspective allows for a broader definition of success, and it emphasizes creativity over conventional achievements like wealth or status. These early narratives can either empower people to pursue their passions or constrain them with rigid definitions of success. It is crucial to reflect on how family stories have influenced our personal aspirations and mindsets.

As we grow, our relationships continue to shape our understanding of success. Friends, colleagues, and mentors play a significant role in defining what success looks like and how it can be achieved. People often find themselves comparing their achievements to those of their peers.

These comparisons can create feelings of inadequacy or motivation, depending on one's perspective. For instance, witnessing a friend land a dream job might inspire someone to pursue their own ambitions, but it might trigger self-doubt in another or make them feel less than.

Assess where you're at in your life right now. Have you ever experienced this? I want to reinforce the importance of being part of a supportive network and how relationships can foster more success. Join groups that celebrate individual achievements, regardless of their nature, because this will encourage your personal growth.

Remember, community reminds us that success is not a zero-sum game. When one person succeeds, it opens doors for others as well. Success is often dotted with both triumphs and struggles. These experiences not only shape our understanding of success but also our resilience and determination. So, next, I want to look at overcoming obstacles.

Consider someone who's faced challenges, such as health issues or financial struggles. Overcoming these obstacles on the way to success might also lead to a deeper appreciation for the process. Success, in this case, is not just about reaching a destination. It's about the strength gained through adversity, sharing the story, and removing the shame from it.

Do not let anyone define your personal success. As we navigate our personal journeys, we often arrive at destinations that might differ from societal norms or even what we expected. Someone who initially might've sought out a high-powered corporate career may realize that true fulfillment comes from serving their community or pursuing an art or passion. Such shifts in perspective require bravery and the willingness to redefine what success means. I previously stated that such shifts in perspective require not only bravery but also a deep willingness to redefine what success truly means. I refer to this courageous behavior as "embodying the spirit of a lion." Even in the face of fear and uncertainty, you become a fearless advocate for your own growth, willing to challenge the status quo, embrace vulnerability, and pursue your aspirations with unwavering determination. This transformation not only empowers you but also inspires those around you to embark on their own journey of self-discovery and reinvention.

Reflecting on the stories we tell is a powerful tool for understanding our relationship with success. By examining our past experiences and the stories we hold, we can uncover insights that shape our present and our future. I encourage you to journal on what that means.

Write about your experiences, successes, and setbacks and help clarify what your values are and what goals you want to achieve. Practice, practice, practice. Share stories, be vulnerable, and connect, whether through conversation, social media, or community gatherings. Lean into podcasts, listen to others' journeys, be an active listener, and be willing to share and be vulnerable. Ask yourself, "Where am I hiding? What do I not want to claim or share? What experience am I not willing to put forth?" Everything we share provides a new perspective on our current success.

Ultimately, a profound relationship with success intertwines with a sense of purpose and service to others. Anyone who achieves financial success may find greater joy in using their resources to support causes that they care about. This shift emphasizes that success is not solely about a personal journey. It can also uplift others. It's all connected.

You might ask yourself, "What impact do I want to have on my community? What kind of impact do I want to have on my family? What legacy do I want to leave? How can my achievements benefit others?" These reflections can guide your choices and actions and lead to a more fulfilling sense of success in your life.

And I want to remind you that there is no such thing as perfection. Perfection paralysis is real. Many people set exceedingly high standards for themselves, and the fear of not meeting them can create anxiety and potential failure. It's all-or-nothing thinking. Perfectionists often view outcomes in black and white, leading them to believe that anything less than perfect is a failure. This mindset is not only paralyzing, but it also paralyzes decision-making and action.

Next is the fear of judgment and social comparison. When you compare yourself to others, the fear of being judged or criticized can deter you from taking risks or actions. Being concerned about what peers, family, and society think can be immobilizing.

The need for acceptance can lead you to avoid situations where you might fail. As a result, you fear that claiming any form of success is a loss of identity. The truth is that success is about what you claim. When you don't claim it, you don't claim a version and a piece of yourself.

Next is the idea that worthiness is tied to success. For some, their self-esteem and identities are closely tied to their achievements. Consequently, the prospect of failure can feel like a threat to their sense of self-worth. This can lead to avoidance behaviors. The fear of disappointment may create worry about disappointing themselves or others, particularly if they have a history of successful outcomes. This can also create pressure to maintain strategies to combat the fear of failure.

The key to overcoming these beliefs is to reframe failure, shifting it from a negative outcome to a learned opportunity. It's that simple. Recognize that each setback can provide valuable insight for future efforts.

Recognize and reset your relationship with success. Set realistic goals and break large goals into smaller, manageable steps. This makes the process less overwhelming and allows for incremental progress. And treat yourself kindly.

I can't stress this enough.

Understand and be kind about setbacks. Know that every part of this journey is guided. There are no mistakes. There's only what you choose to learn and what you choose not to acknowledge. Everyone experiences failures at some point, everyone, and you can actually use this as rocket fuel. Surround yourself with people who encourage you and push you out of your comfort zone and into a growth mindset. Also, sharing your fears can help alleviate the burden that you've created with the belief that success may not be obtainable.

Focus on and trust the process. Rather than focusing solely on the outcome, celebrate the efforts, growth, and joy along the way. Laugh at yourself. Anything you can foster to make it more joyful and fun—call that in and engage in positive visualization.

There are many techniques out there. I want you to imagine a successful outcome. It is just as easy to imagine a successful outcome as an unsuccessful one. The only thing stopping you is you.

Visualizing a successful outcome can not only help build your confidence and reduce anxiety about potential failure, but it actually produces more success. Embracing a growth mindset shifts your perspective, encourages resilience and a willingness not only to face challenges, but also lights a fire of enthusiasm, and reestablishes the understanding that everything is available to you.

Sit with that for a moment. What if everything is available to you?

Previous negative experiences, past failures, uncertainty, and lack of control—all these things play a part in our success, but they can create a lasting fear. If you are facing this, it can be a significant setback, but I want to encourage you that the apprehensiveness you feel about trying again is just a terror barrier. Minimize it, step over it, and try again.

That's what we do. We try again, and we try again, and we try again. It is not a one-and-done. It is a practice. Our past failures should only lead us to say, "I've tried all this, so what's next?" We must ask new questions to get a new outcome.

I would be remiss if I didn't look at trauma and anxiety as part of the law of success for some. Not only are our past failures associated with trauma or intense anxiety, but they make the prospect of facing similar situations in the future particularly daunting.

Again, we have to change our relationship with them. We have to use that story and say, "Yes, I can hold space for that, but I can also hold space for the success of what I dream and desire. Nothing stops me but me." Our stories do not define us.

Understanding the root of fear can help you address and overcome it. We must understand and meet ourselves where we are. Today is the youngest you're ever going to be. What are you going to do with that? Your story has brought you here.

You're reading this now. What can you take from this and apply to your current dream of something new? What is your relationship to success? The belief that success is not obtainable for you is a lie. The truth is that success is found within yourself. Anchoring your success in external validation only leads to failure. The truth is that success is rooted in your authentic truth. That is where your success is.

Look in the mirror and ask yourself, "What is my relationship with everything that I've created in my life? What do I want?" The mirror reflects inescapable truth. It's raw. It's honest. It's vulnerable. It's you.

I want you to speak to yourself and uncover the conditioning beliefs that you've held up until this point. Once you peel away the lies and reveal the truth underneath, anything is possible. Success is yours. What are you going to claim?

QUESTIONS FOR REFLECTION

What do you want to achieve?

_____

_____

_____

What is your relationship to success?

_____

_____

_____

Has your life up until this point been disappointing?

_____

_____

_____

Are your beliefs serving you or holding you back?

_____

_____

_____

What does success look like to you?

_____

_____

_____

What values are most important to you in your journey toward success?

_____

_____

_____

What impact do you want to have on your community?

_____

_____

_____

What impact do you want to have on your family?

_____

_____

_____

How can your achievements benefit others?

_____

_____

_____

CHAPTER 13
IT STARTS AND STOPS HERE
THE LAW OF FORGIVENESS

"The weak can never forgive. Forgiveness is the attribute of the strong."
~Mahatma Gandhi

When I decided to add the law of forgiveness to the book, I struggled with where I needed to apply it. Then this quote came up for me: *"If you forgive men when they sin against you, your heavenly Father will also forgive you"* (Matthew 6:14).

Whether you believe in God, universal energy, or the divine connection, we cannot fully be connected unless we use the law of forgiveness.

Failing to forgive will block us from all our blessings. It will block us from our abundance. It will block us from the universal laws that dance and allow us to flow with it. The law of forgiveness is a simple one, but we make it complicated because of the stories we create around it.

I saved the law of forgiveness for one of the last chapters because I struggled with it the most. If I had forgiven or known how to forgive versions of myself sooner, if I had known that my relationship with shame was so deep and that forgiveness was the key and catalyst for all my healing, it would've been a simpler journey.

I found my first door opening while reading Louise Hay's book, *Mirror Work: 21 Days to Heal Your Life*. When I found out we share the same birthday, Louise and I, and that my connection with her was much deeper than just me tripping over her book, I recognized that she spoke to me on a soul level. I went back and met myself at every age. I picked up that version of myself, that inner child, and I loved her, and I forgave her, and I was grateful for her because she got me here.

I had a dream about ten years ago where I woke up crying. I grabbed my phone and wrote down what I had experienced. I had met my higher version of myself, and she had thanked me with a peace and understanding that I had never known. She grabbed my hands and pulled me in. I could see the blue door and the curtains blowing in the wind, and as I sat down, she thanked me for every version that I had healed and carried. She thanked me for not dying and not giving up.

She pushed the hair away from my tear-stained face and told me how much she loved me and how brave I was, especially through the years when I'd stumbled and couldn't find peace. The world had torn me up, and I had lived reactively. At times, I had even been cruel.

I now recognize the mechanisms I used to protect the gentle, sweet girl who lived within me, the passionate, happy soul that she was speaking to. That dream changed my life. I don't survive anymore. Instead of fierce boundaries, my tools are now gentle reminders of what I know to be true.

THE TRUTH WITHIN THE LIE

THE LIE: *Their relationship to shame is illuminated in truth. It is not.*

THE TRUTH: *Forgiving every version of yourself will give you immense freedom. Do it now; don't delay. This is non-negotiable.*

Shame will keep you from forgiving yourself. There isn't anything you've done that God hasn't already forgiven you for. As pastor and motivational speaker, T. D. Jakes said, "God is good—all the time. Nothing is worthy of God—God is worthy of me."

It must start with our own personal forgiveness. It's very difficult. Poet Maya Angelou said, "I do not trust people that do not love themselves that say they love me."

I used to take offense at that. I thought, "But they do. They love you." Now I understand exactly what she meant by that. We must reflect on our relationship to forgiveness. One of the most powerful tools of forgiveness is the Hawaiian Ho'oponopono prayer: "I'm sorry. Please forgive me. I love you. Thank you."

This prayer acknowledges one's role in pain. It embraces self-love and gratitude. It's simple, and it is the most powerful prayer I know: "I'm sorry. Please forgive me. I love you. Thank you." It can be applied anywhere in your life.

But what is forgiveness? Understanding forgiveness as a practice rooted in love and compassion is powerful.

Forgiveness has many pros. For one thing, it releases any negative emotions that you might be carrying. It also fosters personal growth and healing, and it creates space for love and compassion.

As for cons, it's often misunderstood as condoning harmful behavior. It can also be difficult. However, I say there's an easy way and a hard way. You can choose to be in the struggle, worry, doubt, and fear. This keeps you in the old story. You must choose to forgive. You must choose to do something differently.

The freedom with forgiveness is exponential. We not only release the person that we're bound to by not forgiving, but we also release ourselves into unimaginable peace. We often hear, "I will never forgive them." The difficulty in forgiving oneself or others is a story we've created, and it's layers of ego trying to protect us from being hurt again. The heart, however, just wants to forgive, expand, and love.

Forgiveness is a gift that leads to new beginnings. The law of forgiveness releases you from everything that binds you. Releasing anger is the only way that we are able to move forward.

First, we must identify what stories we are creating. Where are we angry? Where do we need to forgive? What have we done in our life that we can go back and say, "I didn't know any better, but now I do"? I can forgive that version of myself, and I can hold space for not only healing and forgiveness but also love, connectedness, and expansion.

To clarify, forgiveness is not about justifying actions; it's about releasing judgment. Judgment lives in the ego. It divides; it separates. We've watched it divide families, friends, and countries. What would it look like if we released judgment and held space for healing?

The result of holding on to negativity and clinging to anger and resentment is pure toxicity. The principle that every action has an equal and opposite reaction is powerfully relevant to forgiveness. How easy is it for you to forgive? Do you identify as a victim? Do you harbor shame or anger? Can you forgive yourself? What childhood stories do you carry that you've never shared because of shame or guilt? Is there someone you need to forgive?

This doesn't mean you need to pick up the phone and call them. You can have this relationship with yourself, deeply forgive, and release.

Recently, I was on a photo shoot, and the stylist damaged my hair. The makeup was wrong, too, but she demanded full payment. Everything about it felt wrong. I was frustrated because not only was my hair damaged, my cost for everything had doubled. Instead of treating the situation with love, compassion, and forgiveness, I pushed back and wanted her to forfeit the charge.

It didn't take me long, less than an hour, to reach back out to her and meet her where she was. I paid her fee and asked her to forgive me for my reactivity. Whether she forgave me or not, it ended well because it wasn't about making it right for me; it was about meeting myself where I could forgive her. I released the situation and reset completely, and there was freedom in that.

When someone does not live up to the version of them we have created in our story, we feel let down and that what they've done is unforgivable. Now, this has nothing to do with them; instead, it has everything to do with us and our relationship to self. It has everything to do with our self-worth, self-esteem, and worthiness.

Forgive yourself for not knowing better, and then release. You shall be forgiven. How does that sit with you? Can you adapt that principle? You shall be forgiven. Stepping out of reactivity allows for a more compassionate and loving life. Compassion cannot exist without forgiveness.

This universal law is the one that people struggle with the most. Self-forgiveness is essential, and you must let go of resentment and anger toward yourself and others. You have to reestablish forgiveness if you're in the bind of resentment.

How can you find peace when you're in pain and suffering? Your higher self can guide you in this process. This is not about the other person. This is not about the situation. This is about your relationship with self, forgiveness, and how you hold on to resentment, grief, and negativity. What do you get out of holding on to those things? Have you created a narrative that serves you? Usually, when we don't want to forgive, it feeds a victim role.

What role did you play in the situation? Even if you were the victim, it is never one-sided. Holding on to resentment, grief, or any form of angst only creates more negativity. So, again, every action has an equal or opposite action, and forgiveness allows your life to expand.

Forgiveness is about you and your personal growth. It's about you and your relationship to self. It's about understanding and developing boundaries so you can prevent similar events in the future. It's also about reconciling your anger and hurt so you can stop repeating the story.

How many times have you said, "That is unforgivable?" Watch your words very carefully because your life will follow. I go back to "Forgive, and you shall be forgiven." The lie is often that forgiveness is for suckers. If you forgive, you'll only get stepped on again.

The truth is that the law of forgiveness unlocks a well of abundance that is deeper than you've ever experienced in your life. You want expansion. You want a deeper connection to self-love and abundance. It starts with the universal law of forgiveness.

Write down everything in your life that has been hurtful and made you angry. Also, write down the Hawaiian Ho'oponopono prayer as a daily form of meditation. Engage in self-compassion exercises. That means learning to ask different questions, such as "How can I forgive myself?"

The biggest challenge of my life has been to forgive myself for the impact my migraines had, particularly on my three daughters. For years, they tried to tell me their experience and their truth, and I defended myself. I blurred the lines when it came to using the medicine for physical and emotional pain, and it got very messy. I could've died a hundred times over, and they had to witness this.

How do you meet yourself at that level of shame? Self-forgiveness. By forgiving myself, I could hold space for them, and now they're healing. It was the most difficult place for me to hold space, but when I surrendered to the truth, it opened the door to profound healing and a better relationship that I continue to build with my daughters every day. I no longer have the desire to be right. In fact, the older I get, the more I realize that it's not as important to me. I'm a better listener. I'm a better mom, and when I get called out on things, I simply say, "I can do better. I can do better all the time."

My children are now in their late thirties. When they bring these stories up, I say to them, "Please forgive me. Please forgive me for not knowing better. Please forgive me for that period because when we know better, we're required to do better."

I don't hide from the shame of it, but I must forgive myself daily. I can't change the past. I can only use what I know now and change my relationships with myself and them. If I did not change my relationship to self, I could not change my relationship with them. I would completely defend my position that I was a victim of the migraines without taking and acknowledging the impact it had on my daughters. So, I had to forgive myself for not knowing better.

I had to forgive myself for my choices. Now I can hold space for them without being defensive, without being a victim. I can stay open and hold space.

I'm sorry. Please forgive me. I love you.

Acknowledging the pain of past experiences, undergoing the process of letting go of hurt, and embracing forgiveness are some of the most powerful work you can do. Understand that your higher self can guide you in this process.

I often say that lotuses grow out of the mud. They don't grow in the light. They grow out of the muck and the deepest, darkest places in our lives. Is that where the raw version of yourself is rooted? Where there is light, there are shadows. Shadow work is powerful medicine. It is where we find the light. It also cracked me open to deal with the core fear of abandonment and the safety issue I had.

Everything we do is connected to another story and another story and another story. Write out your hurt and anger. What are they connected to? Practice the Hawaiian Ho'oponopono prayer. Make that your meditation.

Keep it simple. Engage in self-compassion exercises every day and set intentions for forgiving yourself and perhaps someone else. Forgiveness is a continuous practice. It is not a one-time act, but it encourages you to embrace love and compassion for yourself and others. There isn't a deeper well of love and connectedness that can be unlocked in your life.

Where do you resist forgiveness? Where is it too painful to lean in? Let love and forgiveness seep into those cracks. What would it feel like if you forgave just one thing in your life? My call to action for you today is to reflect on your forgiveness journey. Then, take actionable steps not only toward releasing what no longer serves you but also finding what you can replace it with.

Without using the law of forgiveness. We can replace nothing. This universal law not only explores forgiveness but also shows the interweaving of our personal experiences and how we can foster an environment of love, compassion, and understanding as we navigate toward forgiveness. Unless life is stopped, we're always going to use this law. Unless you're perfect, it's always going to need to be applied—and there is no perfection.

So, you can see why this law is avoided more than the others: it takes deep personal accountability. We must be willing to step into the radical truth of our lives and accept it. We do this through forgiveness.

To set a tone of forgiveness in your life, you must open with a heartfelt acknowledgment of its complexity and depth. It is often viewed as a burden or a challenging task, yet it holds the most transformational power.

My connection with this universal law has had a profound impact on my life, and I guarantee that it will be a significant source of freedom in your own life when the weight of not forgiving is lifted.

The more you don't forgive, the smaller your world gets. To change this, ask yourself, "By not using the law of forgiveness, what am I protecting? What do I not want to feel?" When you choose not to forgive, it closes you down. It does not open you up. This is a transformational practice. It is specific to how we speak to ourselves, the phrases that you've told yourself, and what resonates with you now.

So, I encourage you to write down affirmations to flip your story: "I am a forgiving person. I can forgive. I am full of compassion and love." Take ownership. When we say, "I am," it is our first chakra. It is our grounding. It is what we anchor ourselves in. Whether you know it or not, these universal laws are at play at every moment of every day of your life.

My goal is for you to have a better relationship with yourself and others. Earlier, I told you about the Hawaiian Ho'oponopono prayer. Now I want to break down each line of the prayer.

"I'm sorry." That acknowledges your role in the situation. Understand that accountability is part of the healing.

"Please forgive me." That is a plea for compassion, both from others and yourself.

"I love you." Embrace self-love as a foundation for forgiveness.

"Thank you." That means cultivating gratitude for the lessons learned through pain.

Adapting the law of forgiveness in your life means defining what your relationship to forgiveness is. It's not a part of the past but a conscious choice to release the grip of negative emotions. That is a choice you make in the current moment. All your choices are in the current moment. The past does not need you anymore, and the future does not need you yet. The current moment is where we use this law to move forth with freedom and healthier relationships.

One of the primary benefits of forgiveness is emotional liberation from the cycle of reactivity and healing. There isn't an area of your life where you can't recognize where you could have done better. There's a cycle of reactivity in our lives, and there are stories anchored in unforgiveness.

Healing begins with self-forgiveness, but bring in like-minded people who can challenge you and the stories you've been bound by. There isn't a day in my life as a coach when someone isn't cracked open and crying. As they work with me, their level of trust grows, and they share stories that are so precious that I want to foster that love and hold space for their self-forgiveness. I have seen unbelievable transformations happen from using this law.

It is the one that people resist the most because they have shamed themselves and told themselves, "I don't deserve it." When we anchor ourselves in shame, regret, and denial, we create narratives that tell us we will find our value and our forgiveness in the external world. Consequently, we'll say, "I'm sorry," a lot. "I'm sorry. I'm sorry. I'm sorry." It'll be repetitive behavior. We will create scenarios where we call in the same situations where we're the victim.

By addressing self-forgiveness, we can release ourselves from the outcome of stories to come. Understanding is the hardest part of this process, but the common barriers that most people face are guilt and shame.

So, sit for a moment, just 30 seconds. Take a deep breath and release. How can you release self-judgment? This is a critical part of this process. Self-judgment is a prison of negativity that hinders all of your growth. Also, how can you forgive your judgment of others? How can you step in and say, "I forgive myself for judging harshly? I forgive myself for showing up like that."

Holding on to anger and unforgiveness is like carrying heavy baggage; it weighs you down. I want you to think of going through the airport and carrying your suitcases, and they're filled with all of your unforgiveness of yourself.

All that's required to put those suitcases down is choosing to say, "I forgive. I release. I will no longer carry that story. It is not the truth."

The law of forgiveness unlocks a deeper well of abundance than you could know. Forgive yourself: unlock that door, step into that basement, look at everything you've got stored there, and, one by one, unpack each story and forgive yourself for it. The feeling you get is something I can't explain. I can't possibly describe what it felt like when I forgave myself, and the weight was lifted. We can only do this through empowerment through our connection with self and meeting ourselves at the deepest, most vulnerable part.

No one knows you better than you. No one knows your stories better than you. Sometimes, however, we've gaslighted ourselves and do not understand our story.

This is a real come-to-Jesus moment when we have to acknowledge our stories to forgive ourselves for them. This moment of empowerment builds inner strength, resilience, and abundance. In fact, think of the law of forgiveness as a springboard into the quantum leaps of calling in what you want. What blocks you is the suffering, the pain, the hiding, the stories, and being anchored in *"I'm not enough. I'm an imposter."* None of that's true. Forgive yourself for even thinking that about yourself.

I want to stress the importance of recognizing and honoring your pain. This is a valid part of the healing process. By acknowledging your pain, not only have you paved the way for personal forgiveness, but you're going to show up in the world and be more forgiving to others.

This is how we know we're not forgiving of self: we show up in the world with judgment. We're quick to judge. We're quick to have a story about anyone and everyone. Is that you? Do you know someone who shows up and is full of judgment? I want to reinforce the continuous nature of forgiveness, how this universal law is always ebbing and flowing, moving and morphing in our lives.

Again, it's not a destination but an ongoing process. I want you to commit to your overall well-being, and I want to remind you that self-compassion is about treating yourself with the same kindness you would offer a dear friend.

Your call to action here is simple: self-forgiveness. Where do you need to be forgiven? Will you take the time to unpack your stories? Is there something so dark and so tragic that you can't forgive? I'm going to create a forgiveness challenge for you. I'm going to give you 30 days to circulate your relationship with forgiveness, journal about your experiences and reflections, and allow yourself to unpack the stories and the things that you took responsibility for that may not even be yours.

The next area to tackle is perfectionism, and we've touched on this. Those with perfectionist tendencies often hold themselves to impossibly high standards. When they fall short, the resulting self-criticism can inhibit their ability to practice self-forgiveness and self-compassion, preventing them from moving forward.

Holding on to anger, either toward oneself or others, can create a barrier to forgiveness. This anger can feel protective, but it often prevents healing and growth. Unresolved trauma can also complicate the process of self-forgiveness. Many people struggle to forgive themselves, and I've presented several stories here of trauma leading to a cycle of self-blame.

The clash between your self-image and actions you regret can create cognitive dissonance. This discomfort can make it difficult to reconcile past behaviors with a more forgiving self-view. Comparing yourself to others who seem to have done better than you can exasperate feelings of inadequacy and hinder your ability to forgive yourself. "If only I could do it like them." Nope, never going to happen. Release that and forgive yourself for even thinking it.

Societal and cultural beliefs about accountability and punishments can influence how people perceive forgiveness. Some may believe that they must suffer for their mistakes and feel unworthy of forgiveness. Others may not have the necessary tools or understanding of what self-forgiveness entails. They may feel lost or unsure of how to proceed.

The most important thing is to recognize and address these barriers. Trusting that nothing is unforgivable is an essential part of the process.

QUESTIONS FOR REFLECTION

How easy is it for you to forgive?

_____

_____

_____

Do you identify as a victim?

_____

_____

_____

Do you harbor shame or anger?

_____

_____

_____

Can you forgive yourself?

_____

_____

_____

Is there someone you need to forgive?

_____

_____

_____

Where do you resist forgiveness?

_____

_____

_____

By not using the law of forgiveness, what are you protecting?

_____

_____

_____

THE TRUTH WITHIN THE LIE

How can you release self-judgment?

_____

_____

_____

How can you forgive your judgment of others?

_____

_____

_____

CHAPTER 14
THE REDWOOD EFFECT
THE LAW OF DIVINE ONENESS

"The separation between you and me is an illusion."
~ Eckhart Tolle

It only makes sense to end the book with the law of divine oneness, which means we are here to awaken from the illusion of separateness and the realization that we are all connected.

Some of my fondest memories as a child are the times we spent at our cabin at a lake in Northern California. I loved the beach. I loved the air. I loved the waves. I loved the smell of the wood in the cabin. I loved the red ants and the big oak tree I used to climb, but I especially loved the redwood trees. My love for nature started early, with camping trips, fishing trips, beautiful streams, lakes, rivers, oceans, and trees. These memories connect me to the awareness of us all. I still spend an enormous amount of time in nature.

I used to hug trees as a child, which has been proven to lower blood pressure and help our overall well-being. This is now a grounding technique, and it activates all five senses: sight, hearing, smell, taste, and touch. The sensing organs for each of these give information to the brain, which helps us understand and perceive the world around us. We are not so separate from each other, and the brain interprets these signals to help us know how things will taste, how they will look, and how they will feel.

Some say that sight is the first sense because the eye is a highly specialized organ, while the other sense organs are progressively less specialized. I disagree with that, but I will say that as a child, looking up at the redwood trees made me feel a part of something bigger. If you know anything about redwood trees, you know that underneath the ground, they are all connected. They are not sole and separate from one another.

Now, as a child, I knew nothing of this. I knew nothing about the expansion of these trees, that they had an internal system, that underneath they were all connected and feeding each other, that the tree itself was only a byproduct. That's their ecosystem.

THE LIE: *We are sole and separated from each other.*

THE TRUTH: *We are all connected, and we mirror each other's hopes and dreams.*

I often found myself as a child putting my left hand on the tree. Now I know that my left hand is my feminine energy and the palm of my hand is connected to my heart energy.

Placing my hand on that tree connected it right to my heart. The smell of the sea air and the trees triggered unbelievable memories of something I wasn't aware of. I would chew on the pine needles and taste the salty air of the ocean on my lips.

Have you ever gone into a situation where a smell has triggered an enormous amount of memories? To this day, when I drive through the Redwoods on my way to the ocean, I experience everything from age three on, and there is an overwhelming connection of joy and oneness.

This lets me know that I am not alone—not alone in my memories, not alone in all the good things connected with this—and we can call on this connection. Even when life feels chaotic, I can close my eyes and remember the connection, the source. So, I want you to remember that whatever law you're running from, it will chase you, and you need to be still because God created you with a divine connection.

It is a scientific fact that we are designed to renew and connect spiritually. This law not only gives a spiritual dimension to this work, but it lets us know that we are all energetically connected. I want to highlight that the harmony, unity, peace, and belonging that we find in the divine is so essential because the fundamental truth is that everything is energy. The ego is what divides and separates us and makes us feel alone. Its job is to protect you from loneliness. It does not understand that this law transcends that.

This law is not about organized religion. It is not about understanding oneness. It is about understanding oneness with your fellow beings because everything is alive, including those redwood trees. Everything is alive.

Everything is moving, and everything is interconnected. Oneness opens the heart and helps you understand that you are never alone. With oneness, you see the inherent goodness in all beings. It is not selective. It is not judging. It is not dividing. Oneness changes your mindset from separateness to unity, creating expansion.

If you feel right now that you are spinning out of your self-awareness, here's some insight. The more aware you are of this, the more you're going to experience it and the more connected you will feel. I challenge you to connect and observe and then connect and observe again. Any disconnect is something that you have chosen.

You don't need to be standing in the middle of a redwood forest to feel oneness. You can recognize that you are a part of something bigger by focusing on overcoming your limited beliefs and understanding your smallness.

If oneness allows you to see the truth and beauty in everything, what lens do you have on your life right now? Are you connected to the truth and beauty in your life? Are you connected to oneness? Or do you feel alone in the world? Do you often call yourself a lone wolf? What stories have you told yourself?

You have the ability to implement new stories every day. The expansion often happens in moments of solitude when you connect to the source's energy. Do you allow yourself moments of oneness, moments of peace, moments of stillness? When you do, you open yourself to the possibility of feeling joy, gratitude, and awe. So, look up into the vast sky and know you're part of something bigger. Sit in silence on the subway or an airplane and realize you are connected to those around you, that everyone has a story, and that you are probably more alike than you know.

Understand that you are not alone in your suffering, that others share sadness, too, that by belonging to and reaching out to a group, perhaps a grief group, you do not have to choose to be alone, that feeling content and connected and knowing that everything will be okay is a choice. The outcome here is about freeing yourself from the fear, doubt, and worry that keep you in the bind.

The lie here is simple but profound: you are alone. The truth is that you are connected to everything.

I want you to recognize yourself in others and understand that connection transcends nationality, religion, and politics. What is at stake here is ego versus heart energy.

The ego's job is to divide and judge, and it contracts. It gets smaller. Your life gets smaller, leading to stress and anxiety, and this feeds worry, doubt, and fear.

If you want your life to get bigger in its oneness, in its expansion, the heart energy must expand. It grows through service. It grows through connection. It grows through compassion. It grows through our willingness to forgive.

Our mindful practices here are to be aware of ego-based thoughts, continually practice compassion, embrace our journey, and challenge our story. Connect to your purpose. Revisit what drives us at a soul level.

Write out a list right now: "What drives me at a soul level?" Gratitude is our highest vibrational tool, so just as with every other universal law, we're going to incorporate it here.

What are you grateful for about your fellow man? What are you grateful for about being connected? Who can you call in that you love being connected to? What is wonderful about them? The reason for this last question is that they're mirroring wonderful things about you, too.

When in doubt, serve others. When you are at a standstill, lean into service. By serving others, we no longer feel separate from them. It allows us to see things through a different lens.

We are here to awaken from the illusion of separateness. This profound quote captures the essence of the universal law of oneness. It invites us to explore the interconnectedness of all beings in a world that often emphasizes division, whether through politics, religion, or personal ego.

This law reminds us that we are not alone. We are part of something greater. We are part of a greater whole.

I talked about my experience with the redwoods as a child, but I did not fully understand my connection to the oneness and something bigger than me until years later. Now, however, the energy courses through my body. I can meditate and bring myself right back to those majestic trees. I can utilize my five senses. I now realize I was so deeply grounded in nature that it probably saved my life.

Spending most of my childhood in the forest allowed me to belong to something bigger than myself. A lot of healing needed to take place in my life as a child, but I did not know that. I just knew that I did not feel safe.

Amongst the trees, the universal law of oneness engulfed me. While I lay on my back and gazed up at them, it whispered in the wind, "You are not alone." I felt that all was right with the world. Did I know what a profound moment that was? No, but I do now.

This is why it is so important for me to finish this book with the universal law of oneness. I realize now that oneness saved my life.

Many people feel depressed and isolated. They do not feel connected. They do not feel cared for. They do not feel loved. They do not feel forgiven. By leaning in and connecting, we can open the door and connect all of them.

As I grew older, I began to understand that this connection was not just a nostalgic memory but a fundamental aspect of our existence. Science has proven that everything is energy and that our bodies, thoughts, and emotions all vibrate at different frequencies, connecting us to one another and the universe. Connecting to those trees brought me into an awareness and a higher vibration that allowed me to open my mind and expand at a different frequency.

This divine connection is not confined to anything anchored in it but encompasses all beings. When we realize that we are part of a larger web of life, we begin to understand that our ego creates the illusion of separateness. Those trees know that they're there to survive with one another.

In California, we recently had one of the largest forest fires to date. It was right in my backyard, and when it happened, we lost many redwood trees. Five years later, at the top of a burned tree, I saw green growth. Now, how could that be possible? The tree was scorched. The answer is that, underneath, it was alive and connected to all the other trees, which were sending nurturing love to it and healing it.

How can we do this? How can we reflect this in our own lives with our neighbors, friends, communities, partners, children, and animals? What is it you are connected to where you can connect healing and growth and know that what you say and do matters? There is never separateness. That is your illusion.

We are all connected. Our energies, bodies, thoughts, and emotions are all connected. The divine connection is not confined to organized religion but transcends it, encompassing all beings. When we realize that we are part of this, we no longer feel alone and isolated. My desire for the world is that we honor and accept the oneness so we can remove judgment and healing can begin.

The shift from a mindset of separateness to one of unity is transformational. Maybe I'm ahead of my time, but I don't think I'm alone. When we open our hearts to the idea of oneness, we begin to see the inherent good in all beings. The more we are aware of connections, the more we experience love, joy, and compassion and want to pay them forward.

In my work, I've observed a common theme with my clients: the desire for deeper connection. Even those who vocalize feelings of isolation or loneliness are inherently seeking to reconnect. This need for belonging drives us to look beyond ourselves and recognize that we are part of a collective human experience. Whatever it is we desire, whatever universal law that we're activating, we must heal. We must recognize that we are connected to it all, that the illusion is a separation, and that recognizing that we are part of something larger can lead to profound awareness.

When we focus solely on ourselves, we limit our experiences and understanding. Our awareness gets smaller and smaller, contracting and contracting, until we are looking through the eye of a needle. However, embracing the concepts of oneness allows us to appreciate the beauty and truth in everything around us without using a lens of judgment.

Moments of solitude can grant you access to this universal energy. So I encourage you, whether it's in the serene beauty of a sunset, the redwoods, or the ocean, or amidst the sounds of laughter in a crowded subway or the silence of an airplane, these experiences can evoke waves of joy and gratitude. If you allow it, if you choose it, one of your greatest powers is the right to choose.

By acknowledging our connection to others, we free ourselves from worry, doubt, and fear. We stop judging. I heard a story a long time ago about a climber who spent days climbing in Yosemite. When the other campers were too loud while he was trying to sleep, he practiced the law of oneness. He pretended that these people were his friends and he was celebrating with them, loving the laughter and the joy. Instead of saying, "Oh, my God, I can't go to sleep because of their noise," he was grateful that they were having such a beautiful experience, and he floated off to sleep.

How often do we judge our fellow man? This story always stuck with me. Instead of judging, he connected with the other campers. Whether he knew it or not, the law of oneness was there. He was grateful for the laughter, for the joy. He no longer judged that he wasn't getting sleep, but he floated off into a beautiful state of rest due to the fact he celebrated the oneness and the serenity of the connection.

By acknowledging our connection to others, we free ourselves and embrace the joy. We embrace the connection, and there is no fear, doubt, or worry because we have released everything just by our celebration of being connected.

The illusion of loneliness is just that: an illusion. This misconception, though very simple, can have a profound impact on your life. The truth is that we are all connected to everything and everyone, and recognizing this dismantles national, religious, and ego-created barriers, allowing us to replace them with understanding and compassion, starting with ourselves. How can you overcome your story of loneliness and isolation? The answer is to show up and let your freak flag fly as high as you can so you can call in people who love, appreciate, and connect with you.

Ego-driven thoughts lead to judgment and division, and they also cause distress and anxiety. How anxious are you? How distressed are you? Where do judgment and division come in? Can you see the contrast when we open our hearts and expand our capacity for love and service? Can you feel the shift in energy? Can you see the ripple effect that you can create in your life with your connections?

This takes not only radical honesty but radical forgiveness. And we must be truthful with ourselves and what we believe to be true about us. Mindful practices cultivate a deeper understanding of the law of oneness, and once again, I want you to consider incorporating them into your daily life.

You may think this is about the bigger picture, but this is about you. This is about your connection to self and your awareness of your ego-based thoughts. When ego-driven thoughts arise, challenge them and shift to a more compassionate perspective that will allow you to connect with your higher self.

Practice compassion, too. Extend kindness to yourself and others. Recognize that everyone is navigating their own struggles and offer support to others whenever possible. Those connections will expand your world and open doors that you never would have opened prior. Embrace this path that you're on because your path is unique.

Celebrate your experiences and understand that they contribute to the collective tapestry of your life. You are not alone. You have created a tapestry, and everyone you've ever come in contact with has left a thumbprint on it. Think about the people who have made an impact on your life, good or bad.

Take a moment to divide a piece of paper with a line down the middle. On the right side of the line, write down the good interactions you have felt. On the left, write down the negative. Which side outweighs the other? The point of this is to get an understanding of how much ego is showing up versus how much heart energy. This will allow us to step in and address the situation. It's important, too, to extend kindness to yourself first and then to others.

Again, embrace this journey and connect to your purpose. That means revisiting what drives you on a soul level and engaging in activities that align with your values and bring you joy. If you don't know what that is, lean in and ask yourself, "What can I do that brings joy in my life?" If you still don't know, start experimenting.

First, take the risk of celebrating or experiencing joy to understand what brings more. That means stepping over the terror barrier and accepting that we're connected to everything. Say to the universe, "Come in and show me. Help me understand that I'm not alone. I'm calling in my guides to align with the values that bring me joy, and I want to revisit on a soulful level what brought me joy as a child."

Next, gratitude is always, always, always going to be your highest vibrational energy. Use gratitude as a tool for connection. Reflect daily on what you appreciate about yourself and others. This can deepen your sense of oneness with the world and those around you.

Focus, too, on serving those around you. Acts of kindness can create a sense of belonging. How often do you judge organizations on where the money's being sent or what's being done? How often have you stepped up and taken action when it's been asked for? There is always a way, and there is always a need. Ask yourself, "What can I do differently now?"

Think back to a conflict in your life. Did you stay in a state of conflict, or did you move to a state of oneness? What would you do differently now? How connected do you really feel to the world around you? In what areas of your life do you experience feelings of division? What stories have you created about your neighbors or those different from you, and what are they based on? Are they generational? Is it even your true relationship with self, or do you have to challenge that as well? How do you assess your connections to yourself and others? What narratives have you constructed around those connections?

Here are some exercises for cultivating oneness. The first is to practice stillness. Close your eyes and take a few deep breaths. Connect to something larger than yourself. Focus on the energy that surrounds you and the connections you share with others.

Another exercise is to sing along with others. Singing activates your throat chakra, allowing you to step into a higher vibrational energy of your truth. Maybe attend a concert or a gathering where you can sing along to songs that touch your heart. This shared experience fosters a sense of community and connection that you would never experience otherwise.

I want you to observe moments of connection. I want you to take notes, for instance, of when your heart and mind open. Then, I want you to reflect on how those moments feel, how you feel more connected to the world, and perhaps how you feel less alone. I also want you to reflect on conflict.

Think back right now to a recent conflict. Did you remain in a state of division, or did you find a way to move toward resolution and oneness? How can you apply this understanding in future instances and interactions?

This universal law invites us to awaken to the truth of our inner connectedness. Make no mistake. As we embrace this law, we will shift our perspective from separateness to unity, fostering more love, compassion, and understanding in our lives and the lives of those around us. By recognizing and nurturing our connections, we not only create a more harmonious world, but we can create one that's rooted in the profound understanding that we are all part of the same tapestry and existence.

In embracing this truth, I want you to remember that you are never alone... You are never alone... You are never alone. The truth is that we are all connected in this messy life. We can be elaborate in our societal constructions, or we can create barriers that obscure our inherent connections to one another. It is our job to break things down and simplify.

To connect, you must reflect on any stories that you've created. Imagine a more connected life and what that would look like for you. What sensations would you call in? How would it change the life you're living right now? What would the expansion look like?

Quantum physics suggests that everything is interconnected at a fundamental level, influencing one another regardless of distance. This illustrates how separateness is an illusion. Look at ecosystems and how they demonstrate interconnectedness. Every organism plays a role in maintaining the balance of life. When one part suffers, the whole system is affected.

The concept of shifting from separateness to unity can be expanded even further. Many of my clients have undergone significant transformations once they embraced oneness and allowed their egos to relax. Now, we don't want to demolish the ego. We just want to make it smaller so our heart energy can expand and we can improve their relationships and emotional well-being to attract the abundance, expansion, and joy that we desire.

Everyone who comes to me wants a bigger and better life. They also come to me not knowing what they truly desire. They might be lost, but it is our job to explore—and it's my job to ask better questions, like how did they end up here? How are their relationships right now? Where do they need to embrace? Do they realize that their body, mind, soul, and emotional health are their financial wealth?

Moments of connectedness lead to more moments of joy and gratitude, but I want you to actively seek out experiences. Cultivate gratitude and joy. Keeping a gratitude journal is a particularly profound practice. I want you to think of yourself as a gratitude collector: collect moments of gratitude and write them down. Seek out gratitude. Seek out joy.

For clients who haven't laughed in years, we use laughter yoga. It starts by laughing slowly and then a little more and a little more. All of a sudden, they're laughing so hard that every energetic chakra and cell in their body is being activated. Their bodies don't know that there is something very funny going on. They just know that they're responding to the energy and activation of oneness. They just know that they're happy.

At the micro level, small acts of kindness, like a smile from a stage or holding a door for a stranger, can foster feelings of connection. I encourage you to connect on small levels, as such actions contribute to a sense of belonging.

It's also important to look at this in a global context. How do your actions on a daily basis impact your environment, society, circle of people, and even future generations? Think about the role you play in a more connected world.

Perhaps you have children or grandchildren. Think about things that haven't even come into existence yet. How can you hold space for this? Ask yourself, "What do I want? What am I willing to practice in my life?" Look for signs that bring in oneness. It's just like the red car theory we discussed previously. When you start to look for red cars, suddenly, you see them everywhere. The same thing goes for oneness.

The minute you start calling oneness in, the minute you start leaning in and practicing some of these micros, all of a sudden, you will see it everywhere. You'll see signs everywhere of oneness and how you can connect.

The ego creates a narrative of separateness, which leads to feelings of isolation. Strategies for quieting the ego, such as meditation or mindfulness, help you reconnect to your true self.

How can you call in more practices? How can you be more connected? How can you be more mindful of what you need? The answer is acknowledging that loneliness is an illusion, making micro connections, discussing how you can show up today, and doing something kind.

The action can be small. Maybe you open the grocery store door and hold it for someone. When you do, smile to yourself and say, "I just connected. I just did something larger than myself. There was oneness there." Don't overthink oneness.

The COVID pandemic heightened our awareness of our interconnectedness, the importance of community support, the importance of sharing stories of how we come together during challenging times, of how alone some of us felt and how digital connections and the importance of the role of social media are, not only in terms of connections but also in division.

Be mindful of who you're following. Are they authentic connections? Do they make your life better? Or do you feel less than and more separate than ever? Unfollow anyone who makes you feel alone and separate. I want you to stay connected to the source of inclusion.

What are you tolerating? I encourage you to have a deeper connection, even with social media. Ask yourself, "Am I judging this through the lens of not being connected to anyone, or do I get fed soul food every day?

I guarantee you that what I'm connected to out there is soul food every day. It's an inspiration. It's encouragement. I challenge you to seek out authentic connections, undertake a deeper self-exploration, and make a contact assessment.

Do you feel a sense of oneness with the people in your life? What can you do to strengthen these connections? Look, too, at the barriers to connections. How can you dismantle them? Are they real, or do the stories you've created keep you trapped behind them? How can you challenge these stories? One way we know that they are stories is that we have played them over and over again. The truth has not yet happened. We must do something new to experience the truth.

The law of oneness gives you a sense of belonging and connection and can lead you to a more profound personal transformation. It also allows for a more compassionate world. If you want more compassion, you must show up in the world and connect to the oneness of compassion. Explore every connection in your life and recognize that all parts of life are beautiful. Step out of judgment and step into love.

I am not saying you do not need to have boundaries around toxicity, but I am challenging you to connect and ask yourself, "What is this teaching me?" By expanding and providing a more detailed insight, you can create a deeper, more meaningful relationship with oneness that can empower you to break free from the illusion of separateness. You can also learn what you want to call in and be connected to.

Once again, I want you to look at how you show up in your daily life and how you nurture connections, including dating online, community interactions, and everyday social exchanges. Is there anyone who doesn't have a computer or isn't spending time connecting and embracing oneness?

Use your technology wisely, call in meaningful connections, share experiences with others, engage in online discussions that resonate with you, and focus on building relationships rather than just accumulating likes and followers on social media. Reflect on your connections. Look at how you can cultivate empathy and understanding and participate in group connections. Create connection rituals.

Please be impeccable with your words and speak with integrity. It matters in your connection with the world. Don't take anything personally. Offer love and compassion. Don't assume that your story is not their story. In fact, your story is connected to everyone, so show up with love and compassion and always do your best. That means your best is going to change from moment to moment and different from day to day.

Avoid self-judgment, self-abuse, and regret, and allow yourself to use the universal law of oneness. Your heart energy does not want you to be isolated. It wants you to connect to the source, God, the universe, the divine.

This law will dance around you like a flame. The more you call it in, the larger the flame will get.

You are not sole and separate. That is a lie. The truth is that you are connected not only to the stories we've talked about today but to everyone and everything. Look around at your environment right now: you are connected to all of it.

QUESTIONS FOR REFLECTION

Are you connected to oneness?

_____

_____

_____

Do you allow yourself moments of oneness, peace, and stillness?

_____

_____

_____

What are you grateful for?

_____

_____

_____

How anxious are you?

_____

_____

_____

What can you do to bring joy into your life?

_____

_____

_____

How connected do you feel to the world around you?

_____

_____

_____

In what areas of your life do you experience feelings of division?

_____

_____

_____

How do you assess your connections to yourself and others?

___

___

___

Do you feel a sense of oneness with the people in your life?

___

___

___

What can you do to strengthen these connections?

___

___

___

How can you dismantle the barriers to connection?

___

___

___

THE TRUTH WITHIN THE LIE

Are they real, or do the stories you've created keep you trapped behind them?

_____

_____

_____

How can you challenge these stories?

_____

_____

_____

CONCLUSION

Thank you for taking the time not only to read this book, but to explore the universal laws and modalities I've shared here. I also want to emphasize the profound importance of how universal laws can work for you. Throughout my journey, I have explored not only how these laws govern but also how the cosmos of my own experiences have shaped my thoughts, actions, and relationships.

I hope that you will take these insights to heart. By embracing these universal principles, you can cultivate a deeper understanding of the world around you and your place in it. I believe that when we align with these universal laws, we unlock the potential for growth, connection, and fulfillment.

We never want to minimize the role of the ego, but we do want to quiet it. I encourage you to reflect on the truths in your life and how they resonate. Ask yourself, "Where am I lying to myself?"

May this book not only inspire you to seek harmony in the universe but also empower you to create a life of purpose, meaning, and connectedness because we are here to love and to be loved. I envision a future where people recognize their agency and responsibility in not only shaping their lives but their environment, too, because it's about empowerment. It's about encouraging you to take charge of your narrative and trust in the process of your growth and transformation.

I invite you to embrace not only curiosity but deep exploration. Ask questions, seek knowledge, and be open to learning from your experiences. Never stop leaning in. Remember that this path is just as important as the destination and that every challenge up to this point has been an opportunity for growth. Yes, an opportunity for growth.

Ultimately, my wish for you is to find your unique path, guided by these universal laws. May you cultivate a life filled with purpose, joy, and a deep sense of connection to the universe and each other.

I want to thank you again for being part of this exploration, and may your journey ahead be rich with discovery and fulfillment.

THANK YOU FOR READING MY BOOK!

Just to say thanks for buying and reading my book, I would like to connect with you!

Scan the QR Code:

I appreciate your interest in my book and value your feedback as it helps me improve future versions of this book. I would appreciate it if you could leave your invaluable review on Amazon.com with your feedback.
Thank you!

www.ingramcontent.com/pod-product-compliance
Lightning Source LLC
Chambersburg PA
CBHW050242010526
44107CB00032B/1384/J